Programming the

World Wide Web

4th Edition

caused a furore, articles in the newspapers and our governors
don't want that. Go in, make a thorough search, allay public
fear and return to the station. That's what we are going to do!'

Thurston moved to the foot of the rickety stairs and stared
up. Nothing but darkness. He felt beneath his cape for the
truncheon hanging on his belt hook. He wished he had a
firearm, a pistol, anything.

Thurston was frightened. It wasn't the darkness, the filth or
the throat-gagging odours but something else, cold and evil,
lurking in the darkness: something about to shatter that terrible
silence.

They began to climb the stairs slowly, the lantern creating a
pool of light around them. On the first stairwell, Coggins
quietly cursed as fat, bloated rats scurried away.

The higher they climbed, the more fearful both policemen
became. Thurston's face grew damp with sweat. The darkness
seemed to embrace them, promising terrors yet to come. There
was little light. The glass in the windows had long been
smashed and either boarded up or covered in grease-covered
paper. This, torn and tattered, flapped noisily in the night
breeze. From the alleys below a dog barked. Thurston recalled
childhood stories about a howling dog being Satan's herald.

They had reached the third storey, making a thorough search
of each room, when Coggins, forgetting all rank, grabbed his
inspector's arm.

'Listen, sir!'

Thurston, one foot on the next stair, tensed. He was about to
reprimand Coggins when he heard it: an eerie creaking as if
someone further up the house kept opening and shutting a door.

'Come on,' Thurston ordered. His throat and mouth were
dry and he pinched his nostrils at the increasingly foul smell.
Where had he experienced that before? Thurston wiped the
sweat from his cheek with the heel of his hand.

'It's the same smell!' he whispered hoarsely. 'Do you

remember, Coggins, when we exhumed that coffin last summer in St Jude's cemetery at Whitechapel?'

'Is there a corpse here, sir? Pshaw!' Coggins turned away, fighting hard to control his nausea.

'A dead cat or some other animal,' Thurston declared.

He climbed on. The creaking now echoed like a bell through the house. On the fourth stairwell Coggins again grasped his inspector's arm.

'Why are we here, sir?'

'Because we are ordered to be, Constable: that's what happens in the police force. Someone gives you an order and you carry it out.' Thurston hoped his voice and army training helped still his terrors as well those of his young companion.

'Who was Benfleet?' Coggins asked.

'He was a wicked old man who owned this house for years. They say he was a soldier who fought with Wellington in Spain, came back with some plunder and bought this untidy pile. Mad as a March hare, he dressed in a woman's gown, yellow as a canary, with a red kerchief round his head. Now, Constable, Benfleet's safely buried in a pinewood coffin, six feet below the clay of St Giles' cemetery. Someone's playing a game!'

They paused.

'We are coming up!' Thurston shouted up the stairs. 'We are police officers. Believe me, when I put the bracelets on your wrists you will regret tonight's japes!'

His words echoed up the gloomy stairwell but the only answer was that ominous creaking. Thurston continued his climb. As he did so, he recalled the stories about the deceased Robert Benfleet. How he used to live in shabby luxury in a room at the top of the house, drinking his pot of port and rocking himself backwards and forwards in a great rocking chair he had bought from a captain of a ship at Tilbury.

At last they reached the stairs to the attic. The creaking was now louder and faster. Coggins moaned as he saw the faint sliver of light through the half-open door at the top.

'Sir, I don't like this. We should go back. This is a rotten, evil place and it's so cold.'

Thurston had to agree: an icy draught was blowing through the house. His sweat-soaked shirt now clung like a pack of ice against his back. Nevertheless he continued. Coggins, shaking so much he could hardly keep the lantern still, trailed behind. The inspector drew his truncheon. At the top he pushed the door open. Inside, dressed in a gown of yellow with a red kerchief wrapped round his evil face, Robert Benfleet, eyes blazing with hatred, a hideous smirk on his lips, swayed backwards and forwards in his great oaken rocking chair . . .

Five nights later, Inspector Thurston and a large party of constables again gathered on the corner of Brinklow Lane.

The inspector would never forget what he had seen at the top of that hideous old house. He and Coggins had immediately fled. Only when they were down two flights of stairs did Thurston regain the presence of mind to start shouting for help from his colleagues below. Coggins had collapsed and had to be taken by carriage to a doctor on the other side of Oxford Circus. Thurston, forgetting all regulations, had gone into a nearby gin shop where, despite the black looks and muttered curses of those within, he had downed a quart of ale. Only then did he lead his men back to the station. He had filed his report. His superiors had not been amused but Thurston had a name and reputation as a brave and honest officer. The superintendent had growled something about fingering the collars of villains, not exorcising ghosts, and said he would seek advice.

Now Thurston had fresh orders. Twenty constables had been assigned to him while, earlier that afternoon, he had also been told to hire six workmen, armed with picks and shovels, to be at Benfleet's house just after dark. These now stood stamping their feet. Thurston's last instruction was to provide every assistance to the man who came to help them.

Just as the clock of a nearby church struck seven, Thurston heard the clop of horses' hooves. A hackney carriage stopped at the far side of the lane. Thurston raised his lantern and stared at the small, dapper figure who climbed out and strolled towards him.

'This is off limits, sir!'

'I know, Inspector.'

The new arrival drew closer. He was dressed rather quaintly in a black, broad-brimmed felt hat and a long overcoat, his chin and mouth almost covered by the muffler round his neck. His boots were like those of a soldier, ankle high and brightly polished.

The man doffed his hat. He put down the shabby black case he carried, took off his leather gloves and shook the Inspector's hand.

'Oliver Grafeld,' he announced.

'Who?'

'I, I am Father Oliver Grafeld.'

Thurston caught the slight stammer. The man seemed as anxious as he.

'I am sorry, Father, but what are you doing here?'

Grafeld stepped closer. He wore round, thin-rimmed spectacles which gave him an owlish look. His face was youngish, olive-skinned; the gentle eyes blinked up at Thurston who towered at least six inches above him.

'You look surprised, Inspector. Weren't you told I was coming?'

'No, Father, I wasn't.'

Thurston studied this young, soft-spoken priest. Now he was up closer, Thurston could see the overcoat was slightly shabby and the muffler frayed, as was the brim of the hat clutched in his hands.

'Are you a Catholic, Inspector?'

'No, sir. I'm not too sure what I am. I say my prayers and I go to the local church on Sunday.'

'So, you've never attended an exorcism?'

'I beg your pardon?'

'An exorcism!'

The young priest picked up his case. He reminded Thurston of his old school teacher; patient and earnest.

'An exorcism, Inspector, is the blessing of a dwelling, a house, or, indeed, a person, to drive away evil, to purge and cleanse it.'

'I've never been to one of those, sir.' Thurston tried to hide the disbelief in his voice.

The young priest tapped him on the hand. 'I assure you, Inspector,' he said, 'this is not some mummery or trickery from St Bartholomew's Fair. Sometimes it works and sometimes it does not.' Grafeld picked up his case and pointed at the house. 'Will you come in with me?'

'I'd rather . . .' Thurston shrugged. 'Of course I will.' His hand went beneath his cape and touched the butt of the revolver nestling in its holster.

'It could be frightening,' the priest continued. He smiled, pushing the spectacles to the top of his nose. 'But that is trickery. Think of it as fireworks or, as Shakespeare puts it; "sound and fury signifying nothing". Now, tell your men to stay outside. They are not to come in whatever they hear.'

The young priest crossed the lane and, without looking to left or right, went inside. Thurston rattled out a series of orders to the constables. He told the attendant sergeant to deploy his men around the house and followed Grafeld in.

He was amazed to find the priest had already picked up one of the lanterns placed inside the doorway and was making his way up the stairs.

'Come on, Inspector!' Father Grafeld's voice sounded boyish and cheerful. 'Forget the nasty smells, the damp walls and the squeaking rats! We don't need an exorcism for them. Hot water, carbolic soap, a good broom and a pot of paint will take care of all that.'

Thurston followed the priest up the stairs. When they reached the fourth storey, the inspector again experienced a feeling of cold evil, smelt the pervasive stench and heard the ominous creaking from the top of the house.

The young priest paused on the stairwell. He placed his hat on the broad windowsill and, crouching down, unlocked his case.

'I hope I haven't forgotten anything,' he murmured. 'If my sister didn't remind me, I assure you, Inspector, I'd walk out without my shirt on!'

'Listen to that creaking!' Thurston exclaimed.

'Just ignore it, Inspector.' The priest's voice became hard. 'You are a former soldier, aren't you?'

Thurston put his lantern down and nodded. The priest stood up.

'It's just like waiting for the enemy,' the priest said. 'Put your trust in God and don't show fear. Now you've got to help me.'

Grafeld placed a purple stole round his neck. He put his gloves inside the overturned hat and took a small candlewick from his pocket.

'Inspector, be so good as to light that.'

Thurston made to obey then jumped as the door to the garret suddenly slammed shut. The creaking increased and he glimpsed the faint light glowing beneath the door. He tried not to gag at the foetid smell but his hand trembled as he held the match to light the candle.

'Very good, Inspector.' The priest now took a small leather-bound volume from his case. 'It's the *Rituale Romanum*,' he explained. 'The Rite laid down by our Church for an exorcism.'

Thurston stared disbelievingly back. He had very little

knowledge about religion, even less about popish practices. In the army he had met a number of Catholics and regarded them as everyone else did, as eccentrics, members of a foreign religion; to be humoured and tolerated but not taken too seriously.

'Now.'

In the lantern light Thurston noticed the priest's face had paled, a fine sheen of sweat glistening beneath the dishevelled line of black hair.

'It can be frightening,' Grafeld declared. 'But, remember this, Inspector: you are never too sure of what is real and what is in your imagination.'

'I don't understand.'

'Did you see a ghost, because you came to this house fearful of seeing something? That's a possibility. Or did you see an entity which has an existence of its own and is bound to this place?'

'Bound?' Thurston whispered, his eyes going beyond the priest to that terrible door at the top of the stairs. The light was now gone, all was silent. Even the terrible smell had disappeared.

'Evil has been done here.' Grafeld gave a lopsided grin. 'To be honest, Inspector, I am as frightened as you. Each situation is different from the rest.'

'You are frightened?'

'Of course.' Grafeld stooped down and took two small phials out of his case.

'Is this your first time? I mean,' Thurston added hastily, 'you look young.'

'Everyone says that, Inspector. My inexperience is more due to nervousness than anything else. I put my faith in Christ and His Blessed Mother.' He grasped the inspector's hand, his touch warm and soft. 'Believe me,' he added, 'we shall both come out of this well. If you can pray. If you cannot, think of something beautiful: your wife, your children, a picnic on a summer's day. Come, our enemy awaits.'

Thurston, the lantern now hanging from a hook on his belt, carried the candle, cupping the flame with his hand. Grafeld went first, not wanting the inspector to see how frightened he really was, indeed, as he always was whenever his Church ordered him to a place like this. He recited the litany, the invocation to God and His saints. He knew it by heart, which was just as well because the light was poor.

'Kyrie eleison! Christe eleison! Kyrie eleison! Lord have mercy! Christ have mercy! Lord have mercy!'

By the time he had reached the top of the stairs Grafeld felt more confident as he continued the invocation to the Trinity, to Mary, Mother of God, to the great saints of the heavenly court. He paused outside the door.

'Just open it,' he ordered Thurston. 'Go inside, put the lantern down, and the candle on a ledge. Leave and wait out here.'

'Are you sure?'

'Please do it!' Grafeld snapped.

The inspector hastened to obey. As he pulled down the latch the door swung open and a blast of cold, foul air made the candle flame dance. The two stepped inside and Thurston held the lantern up.

'There's nothing,' he breathed. 'Nothing at all!'

'Do as I say,' Grafeld whispered.

The inspector put the lantern down and placed the candle on one of the windowsills. Grafeld heard the door close behind the inspector. He heaved a sigh of relief, knelt in the lantern's pool of light and continued the litany.

'St Francis, St Anthony.'

The air was growing colder. The foul stench of death had returned. Grafeld crossed himself three times and, opening one of the phials, sprinkled holy water with his fingers. The smell in the room made him stop and retch. He thanked God that, as usual, he had fasted for the last twenty-four hours, wryly reflecting perhaps this was why the Church insisted on it. He finished the Litany of the Saints and began further prayers, asking for divine assistance.

Suddenly the door flew open. Grafeld glimpsed Thurston's surprised face before it slammed shut. Again the darkness, the cold and that reeking odour.

Grafeld was halfway through the 'Our Father', stumbling over the Latin words, when he heard the breathing, soft yet rapid, as if someone had run far and was now hiding in the shadows trying to catch their breath. Grafeld concentrated on his prayers. He now accepted that the police had not panicked or embroidered their tale. This place, the entire house, stank of evil. Some terrible act had occurred here. The old man Benfleet had not continued his journey after death but was still trapped in the wickedness he had done.

The breathing grew louder. Grafeld now opened the second phial and traced on his own brow a cross with the chrism, the holy oil of baptism. On his knees he shuffled to the wall and made a similar sign there.

'You foulsome, interfering little bastard! You whoreson dog!' The voice growled low and throaty from the darkness. 'Why don't you piss off, little priest! Why not go back to your toothsome little sister at the boarding house? Why not climb into her bed, you'd like that, wouldn't you? Still grieving over Arthur, are you?'

Silence, followed by a low, menacing chuckle. 'On your knees saying your prayers are you, boy?'

The voice had now moved to a far corner. Grafeld closed his eyes and recited the prayers he knew by heart. Sometimes he'd be distracted: he was with Arthur under that oak tree and the thunderstorm was raging about them and the lightning was falling like fire from heaven. Or Emma on her wedding day in her white satin dress and Oliver, watching her come up the aisle, knew he'd never seen anyone so beautiful. He tried to clear his mind but he couldn't. He closed his breviary.

'In the name of Jesus,' he said softly. 'I command you, by what name are you called?'

'Piss off!'

'In the name of the Lord Jesus,' Grafeld repeated. 'By what name are you called? Why are you here? Answer me!'

'Answer you, answer you . . .?' I don't take orders from nancy boys!'

Again Grafeld repeated his commands.

'If you want to know,' the voice was whining, 'my name is Robert Benfleet, owner of this house. You, little priest, are trespassing!'

The door was again flung open and then slammed shut. As it did, the room filled with light as if gas lanterns had been lit. Grafeld gazed at the terrible figure with its back to the door, the stained yellow gown covering the squat body, the red kerchief round the leering old face.

'Why are you here?' Grafeld commanded.

The room was plunged into darkness. Grafeld returned to his prayers. Creak! Creak! Creak! A rocking chair was being pushed backwards and forwards. Then the lantern moved slowly, carried by some invisible hand, and was put down with a crash. Grafeld stood up. In the faint light, he saw the outlines of the rocking chair and that terrible figure swaying backwards and forwards like a child on a swing.

'I know what you are thinking.' The voice became sing-song. 'Am I dreaming or is this real?'

'Why are you here?' Grafeld repeated. He must not be distracted.

'This is my place.' The voice became low and tired.

'And where do you dwell?'

'In the dead of night.'

'And why do you not go?'

'Judgement, fear of judgement!'

'In Christ's name!' Grafeld declared. 'I bid you leave this place in the Name of the Father, the Son, the Holy Ghost!'

The lantern fell over as if it had been kicked. Grafeld felt himself shoved back against the wall. The door slammed open and shut. There was a pounding on the stairs outside. He heard Thurston yell. A cry came from below like that of some fugitive trapped and caught by his pursuers.

Grafeld continued the exorcism. He blessed each corner of the room, daubing the wall with the sign of the cross, sprinkling the holy water over the floor. The air grew less cold; now the only stench came from the mustiness of the dirty chamber. Grafeld felt hungry and tired. He sat down with his back to the wall. With a knock on the door Thurston entered, carrying another lantern.

'Father, are you all right?'

'I am so hungry and tired, Inspector. What happened out there?'

'I heard noises, voices from the inside here. The door kept opening and shutting then somebody pushed by me. I was nearly knocked down the stairs as if someone was running away.' Thurston smiled weakly. 'Being a policeman I gave chase but there was nothing. Could it return?'

'Possibly,' Grafeld replied. 'But, if it does, it will be weaker, at least for a while, and, Inspector, that's where you come in.' He pointed to the hearth. 'Can I ask a favour?'

'Anything you want, Father.'

'Could one of your men light a fire?'

Grafeld hitched his coat up. Thurston heard the jingle in his pocket.

'You want some food, Father?'

'I'd love a pie and a mug of tea. We are not yet finished here, Inspector.'

Thurston hurried off, only too eager to bring more constables into the house. Kindling and some coal were found and fires were lit in the scullery and in the attic. Another constable brought up tea and sandwiches of beef dripping from their supply wagon. Grafeld bit into the bread.

'It's rather stale,' Thurston explained. 'The tea is strong but . . .'

'Pure ambrosia,' the priest replied. 'Now, Inspector, this house has a small garden at the back?'

'More of a yard really.'

The priest took another mouthful.

'And, here in the attic, the walls are thin. You found coal and kindling in the cellar?'

Thurston nodded.

'Then logic dictates,' Grafeld went on, 'that it must be the cellar. Send your men down there, tell them to dig as deep as they can.'

'What are you looking for, Father?'

'The bond, the chain which kept Benfleet's spirit here.'

'You are so sure?'

'It's always the same. Whatever you may read in the penny dreadfuls, ghosts do not haunt houses, gardens or streets because they have taken a fancy to them. It's always something else, be it confusion, ignorance or, in this case, evil. If you search hard enough, you always find it.'

Thurston pulled a face. He really couldn't believe what had happened here. Then he remembered that dreadful figure, the stench, the coldness, the low mocking voice from the other side of the door and decided it would be best to humour this strange priest.

Thurston clattered down the stairs shouting orders. Grafeld finished his tea and the last of his sandwich. He remembered he had said no prayer of thanks and wearily got to his knees to do so. Nevertheless, he was still distracted. He wondered if

Emma was asleep or up worrying about him? She had done so ever since they had moved from their parish at Barking. From below he heard the faint sounds of digging and the shouts of the constables.

'Let's go at it pell mell,' Grafeld whispered. 'To Heaven or, hand in hand, to Hell!'

He put his breviary, the phials of oil and holy water back in the battered case. He crouched before the fire, his stomach rumbling.

'Things sweet to taste prove indigestibly sour,' Oliver quoted from his favourite Shakespeare play, *Richard II*. Perhaps tea and beef dripping did not mix so well?

The room was growing warmer. Grafeld's back was aching so he sat in a corner, crossed his arms and was fast asleep when Thurston came back into the room.

'Father Grafeld! Father Grafeld!'

Grafeld opened his eyes.

'I've been wasting your time, Inspector?'

Thurston's face was grim. 'No, far from it. We've only been digging for an hour and found three corpses. The cellar is large and cavernous, there are bound to be more.'

Grafeld struggled to his feet.

'You knew there'd be something, didn't you?'

'Yes, as I said,' the priest replied, 'there always is. Do you read Shakespeare, Inspector?'

Thurston shrugged.

'Shakespeare knew what he was writing about. In every one of his plays, whenever a ghost appears, it is because of evil unresolved: that's as true of Elsinore in Denmark as it is of the Seven Dials in London.'

Chapter 2

At Candleton Hall, which stood in the ice-bound countryside of Norfolk, Lady Alice Seaton was locked in her own nightmare.

She was standing outside the Hall. A group of riders was milling about, ready for the hunt; the crisp, cold air was broken by the yapping of dogs and shouts of the whippers-in. Her husband, Sir Thomas, was sitting on his great roan, a large cup of claret in his hand. He was toasting himself and the other hunters. Now and again he'd shoot an angry glance at her. Horns sounded, the dogs gathered. Lady Alice, in her dream, watched the hunt stream out over the fields, the bell-like barks of the dogs filling the valley. She then walked back into the Hall but, when she opened the door, instead of the lights, the carpets, the wall hangings and pictures, it was empty and cold like a mausoleum. At the top of the main staircase figures clustered, shadowy and sinister. Lady Alice tried to go back but the door was locked. The figures, gliding like tendrils of mist over the mere, floated down towards her.

Lady Alice woke with a start, her hand going out to where her husband should lie. The bedside was cold.

'God have mercy!'

Lady Alice sat up and put her face in her hands. Thomas had been dead now for almost three months, killed when that great roan had misjudged a hedge and sent his rider tumbling into a neck-breaking fall.

She glanced across her spacious bedroom. The curtains of the four-poster were tied back. She had insisted on that because, when the nightmares woke her in the dark, she felt as if she were lost, buried in that deep, dark crypt beneath the church.

The fire behind its wire mesh still glowed cheerfully and the night lamp on the table mid-way across the room afforded some relief against the dark.

Lady Alice pulled herself further up against the bolsters, listening to the sounds of the old manor house. She had been at Candleton twenty years and loved the Hall. She knew every creak and groan of its ancient timbers. Once upon a time she had loved to wake in the early hours and wander around but not now, not recently. Lady Alice played nervously with the cord which tied the neck of her nightgown. Leaning forward she peered at the clock on the mantelpiece; as she did so, the church clock began to chime three o'clock in the morning.

Perhaps this time she had slept through the visitation, it might be a trouble-free night? As if in answer to her fears, footsteps sounded in the long gallery outside: slow, ominous, light yet threatening. She threw back the covers, swung her legs off the bed. She winced at the discomfort in her stomach and, for a while, fumbled for her warm woollen slippers. She grasped the ash cane and made her way to the door. The gallery outside was cold; small oil lamps provided pools of light. Strange, Lady Alice thought, at the height of summer, with the sun streaming through the rose window at the far end of the gallery, this was a golden place full of light and dancing sunbeams. Now it was a place of shadows and dark, indeterminate shapes.

Lady Alice swallowed hard and cursed her own imagination. She knew the servants were talking. Rumours were growing that something wicked had come to Candleton. She strained her ears for the footsteps but there was nothing. Summoning up her courage and grasping the cane, Lady Alice walked along the gallery. The walls on either side bore weapons, armorial escutcheons, portraits of Sir Thomas's ancestors, hunting trophies, the bric-à-brac accumulated over the centuries. The carpet underfoot was thick and soft. Lady Alice stopped. She was scarcely making a sound yet, when she crouched on her bed, those footsteps sounded as if there were no carpet.

Lady Alice reached the top of the stairs and stared down. No light shone in the hallway below. Lady Alice turned and, as she did, heard footsteps, sharp and clear, as if someone was coming down the gallery to meet her. She crossed herself and, swinging the cane, walked bravely back to her bedchamber's half-open door. The sound of footsteps faded. She was about to dismiss it as a figment of her imagination when they began again, this time behind her. Lady Alice whirled round.

'Who are you?' she called. 'For God's sake, answer me!'

Her voice echoed hollow. Lady Alice reached the bedroom door and grasped the handle.

'What was that? What was that?'

The voice was a woman's and came out of nowhere. Lady Alice turned. The gallery was still dark and empty; her hand flew to her lips. Her fingers were wet and sticky with blood from the handle she had touched. Lady Alice grasped it again then brought her hand away, this time with more blood.

'What's that? What's that?' The voice was sharp and piercing.

Lady Alice was pushed aside as if someone, running down the hall, had knocked her shoulder. She crashed against the door, bruising her arm and, without a second thought, she threw herself into her bedroom, locking the door behind her. When she splashed water over her fingers at her wash stand, the blood promptly disappeared. She lit some more candles and sat on the edge of her bed. She wished that, as at her house in London, gas had been brought to the Hall so, with every light on, she could examine each nook and cranny.

'Am I going mad?' she whispered. 'Is this guilt?'

Lady Alice knew in her heart of hearts she had taken too much. She had explained as much in the letter written to her good friend Archbishop Manning. It was not just the terrors of the night or the phantasms of the dark. No hour, no time, no place was now safe. She would be cutting flowers in the garden behind the Hall and, looking up, glimpse a shadowy figure standing in the corner. She'd gone down to cut some rushes in the mere and, when she had heard a sound, looked up and glimpsed a figure, dark and cowled like that of a monk, standing in the flat-bottomed barge moored there. Or in the afternoon, checking the accounts or talking to her steward and bailiffs, she'd go to the window because she loved to watch the sunset and see, ever so distinctly, a woman in medieval gown and head-dress staring balefully up at her.

Lady Alice went to pull back the curtains. The pale light of the full moon revealed a faint showering of snow along the pebble-dashed driveway. She could just about make out the faint, dark outline of the manor chapel and the high curtained wall which bounded the old graveyard. Lady Alice was about to turn away when she noticed two pinpricks of light on the top of the cemetery wall as if someone had placed candles there.

'What on earth!' she gasped.

The lights suddenly rose, dancing for a while in the night air before coming together to form one flame. For a while the flame just burnt and glowed like a torch, then it moved like a fire arrow, but slowly, through the night air towards her. Lady Alice's throat went dry, her legs began to shake. She felt so cold. She couldn't believe her eyes: nothing like this had happened before! The mysterious tongue of flame was now moving faster. She let the curtain drop and retreated back to her bed.

I am dreaming, she thought, I am in a nightmare.

Just when she had thought this figment would disappear, the tapping began at the window, long fingernails rapping against the mullioned glass, insistent and noisy. Lady Alice sprang to her feet and tugged at the bell rope. The tapping grew louder, threatening to crack the pane. She could bear the tension no longer. She screamed; the tapping stopped. Then Lady Alice heard footsteps outside, the same as before, followed by a rapping on the bedroom door. She ran towards it and tugged at the handle but the door wouldn't open.

'I can't!' she cried. 'I can't!'

She grasped the handle again. This time it turned. Lady Alice flung the door back. The woman outside was the one she had seen before: a dark veiled wimple round her hair, a brown smock over a silken chemise, its collar stretching up under her chin. Lady Alice stared in terror at the liverish face, those glaring eyes, the lips curled like a dog. She slammed the door shut, her last conscious act before she fell into a dead faint.

'Ah, Father Grafeld, Miss Grafeld, do come in. The Archbishop is waiting for you.'

The housekeeper placed the priest's hat and umbrella on a stand just inside the doorway but, instead of leading the visitors to the parlour on the right, she took them upstairs. Halfway up she turned, her dumpy face creased into a smile.

'The Archbishop usually sees his guests in the parlour. God knows why but he's told me to take you up to his personal study.'

Oliver turned to his sister and raised his eyebrows. They followed the housekeeper up at least three flights of stairs before being ushered into a spacious room. A fire burnt vigorously in the marble fireplace; the curtains were drawn. Gas lamps glowed and every inch of wall was covered with shelves full of leather-bound volumes. The Archbishop was standing at the window, pulling back the curtain, watching the carriages rattle along the street below. For a while he stood there, a tall, portly man, his long frock coat buttoned up.

'Your guests, your eminence!'

Manning looked over his shoulder and smiled.

'Thank you, Mrs Appleton.'

He waited until the housekeeper closed the door behind her,

then went to stand behind his desk. He beckoned Oliver and his sister forward, shook their hands and gestured at the black leather armchairs.

'Please do sit. I have just been watching the weather. It's eleven in the morning and the frost still hasn't melted. The almanac says we will have snow by Christmas.'

The Archbishop had been told that he had a broad, honest face. He tried to complement this with a bluff, hearty manner but his two guests did not simper, smile or hasten to agree.

The woman sat in her armchair, her bonnet tied tightly under her chin. She wore a dark maroon coat, the top button of which was undone, and the Archbishop glimpsed a black dress beneath the starched white collar. A very pretty face, the Archbishop considered: well-chiselled features, large sea-grey eyes, a slightly snub nose, generous lips but a determined set to her chin. With black curly ringlets peeping out from beneath her bonnet, Emma Grafeld reminded Manning of a china doll he had on his mantelpiece in the parlour below. A pretty young thing, he decided, but stubborn and determined.

Her brother was darker skinned and his clothes seemed ill-fitting, the white stock beneath the black overcoat slightly scuffed while his black hair was ruffled, tinged with grey above the ears. Manning coughed and stared up at the ceiling before giving the young priest another quick glance. Youthful, he judged, rather innocent. Now and again Grafeld would blink and narrow his eyes; Manning wondered whether his eyesight was poor.

Whatever the reason, the Archbishop definitely felt uncomfortable. He ran his finger round his white stock collar, patted the purple vest beneath the coat then suddenly remembered his manners.

'I'd tell you to take your coats off but it can be rather cold.' He leant over and pulled a bell rope.

Mrs Appleton appeared immediately: she knew the

Archbishop and had not bothered to go downstairs.

'You'd like some coffee, your eminence?'

Manning glanced at his visitors.

'That would be very nice.'

Emma Grafeld's tone was sharp and incisive, her eyes never leaving the Archbishop's face. Mrs Appleton closed the door behind her. Manning squirmed in his chair, steepling his fingers before his face. He only wished his two visitors would make some conversation and not just stare at him.

'Your eminence.' The young woman struggled to sit more formally in the armchair. 'Your eminence, have you brought my brother here to offer him a parish?'

Manning took his hands away and sighed. He knew such a question would arise. He had studied the file on this extraordinary young priest and felt rather sorry for him.

'I appreciate,' Manning began, 'that your brother, well he's been moved from church to church, from house to house, but he . . .'

'But he has been an exorcist, your eminence, that's what you are saying. My brother came from Valladolid five years ago. He was ordained, here in London, by your predecessor Cardinal Wiseman.'

'I know what your brother has done.' The Archbishop's bonhomie disappeared. 'He is a young man, educated and ordained for the Church. He has special talents and gifts. My predecessor appointed him, despite his youth, as the exorcist in north London.'

'We live out of chests and boxes,' Emma replied tartly. 'Taken to the most dreadful places at the dead of night!'

She glanced angrily at her brother for support. However, Oliver was lost in a reverie, his eyes fixed on a far corner behind the Archbishop: his hand had slipped into his overcoat pocket where he kept his rosary beads. Emma swallowed hard. You are a child, she thought, so innocent, so naïve.

'I have not brought your brother here,' Manning intervened, 'to talk about a parish. My invitation was to him.'

The Archbishop could have bitten his tongue off but the words had rushed out. The young woman blushed and stared down.

'Your eminence.' Oliver drew himself up. 'Your eminence, I apologise but . . .'

'I know,' Manning intervened. 'I shouldn't have said that.'

He paused as Mrs Appleton returned and served cups of coffee and plates of biscuits. For a while all was confusion as the housekeeper, muttering under her breath, moved small tables up beside each armchair.

'Thank you, Mrs Appleton.'

Once the door was closed the Archbishop decided to manage the meeting better. He opened the file on his desk, allowing his guests to sip at their coffee.

'You are Oliver Grafeld,' the Archbishop began. 'Thirty-two years of age. Your father was a soldier, then a yeoman farmer in Sussex. Your mother was of French nationality. Both your parents were Catholics. At the age of sixteen you expressed a desire to become a priest and, after attending the local grammar school in Horsham, you were sent to the English college of Valladolid in Spain.' The Archbishop glanced up. 'You received excellent reports from the rector: he describes you as a very good scholar, winning prizes in theology, logic and philosophy. Your treatise on exorcism in the New Testament was published by journals in France, Spain and Italy. You are described as personable.' He smiled at the young priest who was staring at him owlishly. 'That is the good news,' the Archbishop murmured. 'Oh, it goes on. You are described as a man of prayer, devout but absentminded, which sometimes can be taken as lacking in care and compassion for your fellow man. Your sermons.' The Archbishop waved a hand. 'Well, your sermons,' he finished tactfully, 'are not of the same high standard as your writing.'

'My brother is shy,' Emma broke in. 'When he was young, he had a stammer.'

'Your brother is a priest,' the Archbishop retorted. 'His job is to work amongst the people of Christ.' Manning's eyes softened; Father Oliver looked distressed. 'I think you are just absentminded,' Manning went on. 'You have caused consternation by turning up on the altar to celebrate the sacrifice of the Mass, often forgetting to robe according to the liturgical canon.'

Emma made a rude sound with her lips. The Archbishop chose to ignore this as a splutter after drinking hot coffee.

'You can be silent and withdrawn,' the Archbishop continued. 'Conversation with you can be positively embarrassing. But, once relaxed, you talk animatedly. You have a passion for medieval history and Shakespeare. You are a good priest: there is no hint of any evidence to the contrary.' The Archbishop picked up an envelope from the file and shook out its contents. 'You also have a remarkable gift. The rector of Valladolid brought this to the notice of the Church authorities at every stage in your training. Perhaps, Father Oliver, you would like to explain this gift?'

The young priest was still staring at the far corner of the room.

'Father Oliver? Perhaps you'd like to explain?'

Emma made to intervene but the Archbishop held his hand up.

'I see things,' Oliver replied. 'I have, ever since I was a boy, been able to see things other people cannot.'

'What things?' the Archbishop asked testily.

'I can sense atmosphere. I can go into a house or a room. If there is something invisible, unknown to others, I can see or sense it.'

'You mean ghosts?' The Archbishop tried to keep the irony from his voice.

'If your eminence says so!'

The Archbishop was surprised at this apparently gentle young priest now snapping back. He recalled another line from Grafeld's file describing how, on occasions, he could be stubborn to the point of obstinacy.

'As you say, your eminence, we all have our gifts. Some people can talk and enthrall their audiences. I saw George Macready playing Macbeth.' Oliver closed his eyes and sighed. 'Brilliant! The man was truly brilliant! You know, your eminence, that last speech about all our yesteryears . . .?'

'Yes, yes,' the Archbishop broke in. 'I know your enthusiasm for Shakespeare but we were talking about your gifts.'

'It's hard to describe. You enter a room and you can see things as they once were. It's like going into a church after solemn High Mass: the candles are doused, the church is in darkness but you can smell the incense, still hear the singing, sense the chanting, the light, the gorgeous ritual.'

Manning nodded. He had felt this on many occasions.

'Now, what happens?' Oliver continued. 'If you could also see forms and shapes of what had been?'

'Does this happen every time?'

'No. In fact, far from it. The presence must be strong.'

'Yet there's no mention of ghosts in the Gospels?'

Oliver leant forward. 'I am sorry, your eminence, but you are wrong. When Jesus walked on the water, His disciples thought He was a ghost. After the resurrection Jesus had to reassure His followers that it was truly He.'

'But surely, after death the soul goes immediately to God?'

'Your eminence, we do not know what death is. Jesus talks of it as a journey going back to the Father. Walter Raleigh, before he was executed in Westminster Yard, said he had a long voyage to make. Other great thinkers have also described death as travelling on. But what happens, your eminence, if a soul dies and cannot or does not want to leave? You have been in a railway station. The locomotive arrives and the passengers get out of their carriages. Some walk away immediately; some are confused. Others stand still: they want to remain with something familiar before they go forward.'

'Like a baby clings to his mother?' Emma put her cup down and joined in the conversation.

'I beg your pardon?' Manning said.

'When a baby is born,' Emma explained, 'he begins a journey through life. At first, he does not wish to leave his mother's womb and, when born, clings to her.'

Manning narrowed his eyes. He would have to watch Emma Grafeld. She would be a matter he intended to broach with her brother.

'And you say this is how hauntings occur?'

'I think so,' Oliver replied. 'The spirit, whatever that is, the intelligence and will of a person, may not wish to leave. He or she could be frightened, confused, unwilling to move on. Or.' He paused.

'Or what?'

'It could be more determined and self-willed: tasks not finished; debts not paid; justice not done.' Oliver breathed in. 'In some cases it might be terrible evil. The dead person knows he or she has done wrong so they are frightened to make the journey, or cannot, until that evil is resolved. Shakespeare makes great play of that.'

'The ghosts of Macbeth's victims?'

'Precisely, your eminence. It makes no difference whether it be the halls of Glamis or the Seven Dials in London.'

'Yes, I heard about that.' Manning went back to the file. 'Eleven corpses were unearthed. They believed Benfleet was a great killer.'

'Benfleet committed evil acts. That evil held him back.'

'And yet.' Manning looked down at his notes. 'Inspector Thurston claims that there were voices, movement, even Benfleet himself. These materialisations: it's difficult to accept.'

Oliver shook his head. 'Your eminence, I am no scientist. My knowledge of physics is to pay lip service to Master Newton and the other mathematicians. However, we know that the intellect and the will can achieve great things. When you pray all you do is use your lips but if the mind, the heart and the will are centred on something, it will happen. Christ says that faith can even move a mountain.'

Manning noticed how the priest was becoming animated. He now sat on the edge of his chair, his whole body betraying what he so passionately believed in.

'It's like a painting, your eminence. It's not the eye or the hand which executes a great masterpiece, it's the intellect and the will. If it wasn't, anyone of us could be a Rembrandt.'

'And Benfleet?'

Manning felt a little embarrassed at being lectured by a simple priest yet fascinated all the same.

'Benfleet died but his vital part, the soul, the mind, the will survived. These could break through, perhaps even batten on the evil he had left behind.'

'It is so hard to believe.' Manning leant back in his chair. He looked at his cigar case and wished he hadn't promised himself not to smoke until dusk.

'I mean, Father,' the Archbishop continued, 'here we are at the end of 1865. In America their civil war has just ended where hundreds and thousands of soldiers died due to new armaments and weapons. We have steamships, railways, factories and sprawling cities which, only a few years ago, were villages. Science makes advances by the day and all we believe in is turned on its head. Darwin cast doubts upon Genesis. And the devil?' Manning pulled a face. 'Is about as frightening as Punch and Judy.'

'But the spirit world exists,' Oliver argued. 'Indeed, your eminence, I believe that science will prove, not disprove, that two realities can exist together. We know that by prayer and thought we can enter the spirit world. Must we think it surprising that the spirit world, when it wishes, can respond?'

'Ah yes,' Manning replied, eager to show his authority; he wagged a finger. 'Spiritualism and mediums are the rage of our society. The Church's teaching is quite clear . . .'

'My brother does not meddle in spiritualism,' Emma retorted tartly. 'My brother is told to go from one place to another. To visit evil places like Seven Dials when he should have a parish, a presbytery, a stipend of his own.'

'But you have a house.'

'I left my house,' Emma said. 'You should know that, your eminence. My husband was a corporal in the Black Watch. He died in India.'

'Ah yes.'

'My brother is now my care.'

'Tongues can wag.'

'No, your eminence, tongues *will* wag. I can't live my life fearful of spiteful gossip. My parents are dead. We have no kin. My brother is my family.'

Oliver went to intervene but Emma pressed him back in the armchair.

'If there's no opportunity of a presbytery, no parish, why is my brother here?'

'I'll come to that.' Manning scratched his head testily. 'Some further points, Father. You say that in your exorcism of these hauntings you actually see, hear or feel phenomena?'

'Of course! They are in the reports I always make.'

'And you are sure they are not in your imagination?'

'Part of them are!'

'I beg your pardon?'

'Your eminence, we all perceive things differently. Even a vision is tempered by what we feel or think.'

'So, the Virgin Mary did not really appear at Lourdes?'

'I did not say that. I have read the reports about the visionary

29

Bernadette Soubirous. She, undoubtedly, saw the Virgin but her vision is tempered by her own mind, background, experience and upbringing. It's true of the visionaries in the past. In the seventeenth century St Margaret Mary in France saw Christ as her loving Lord. Teresa of Avila wrote about him as . . .' Oliver stumbled. 'As a woman would about her lover. Yet they are both real.'

Manning decided not to pursue the matter but coughed and stared across the room. He felt slightly ridiculous. Here he was, leader of the Church in England, sitting in this stuffy study discussing ghosts and exorcisms with a young priest and his firebrand of a sister. It would be tempting to dismiss Grafeld as one of those many cranks the Church had to suffer yet Grafeld was a good priest. He followed the *Rituale Romanum*; he was discreet and did not boast or seek notoriety, even though it often pursued him in the form of news-hungry journalists.

Manning picked up the file and shuffled through the papers. There were other references here he would love to probe. Something the seminary had said about his dead brother Arthur and a terrible accident which had occurred when the priest was a boy. Nevertheless, Manning believed he had questioned enough. He glanced quickly at Grafeld; the young priest was staring into the corner behind him.

'Any questions, Grafeld?'

'Your eminence?'

'You seem ill at ease?'

'Your eminence, why did you bring us here? No, I mean this is a spacious house. You have parlours and studies below?'

'I wanted to be discreet.'

'You are my Archbishop. I am a simple priest.' Oliver's voice took on a stubborn tone. 'I do not wish to call you a liar.'

'I beg your pardon, Father!'

'You say you brought us up here,' Oliver declared, 'because it is more discreet. However, I suspect Mrs Appleton is listening

at the door outside as she would have done downstairs.'
Manning became more guarded.
'And?'
'Your eminence, why are you testing me?'
'Testing you?'
Oliver put his hand out to placate his sister.
'Oh yes, your eminence, this room is haunted, is it not?'

Chapter 3

Manning shuffled in embarrassment.

'That's why you brought us here wasn't it?' Oliver insisted. 'I do not wish to be smug but, even if I hadn't sensed something, I would think it was strange.'

'What do you sense, Father?'

Oliver shrugged. 'This is a very comfortable study. The leather-bound books, the wainscoting, the crackling fire, heavy curtains and carpets. A peaceful place, but the presence,' he pointed behind the Archbishop, 'comes from over there as if someone sobs in the shadows. It is not harmful, dangerous or threatening but deeply unhappy.'

'Remarkable.'

Oliver blinked at the sarcasm in the Archbishop's reply.

'Is it, your eminence? Haven't you ever sat in a confessional? You hear the door open on the other side. The person kneels behind the grille: you can always tell when something special, extraordinary or tragic is about to unfold.'

Manning smiled at Emma, who was glaring. He spread his hands.

'Father, I apologise. I was curious. Yes, I believe the room is haunted. It's nothing remarkable. When I am alone, sometimes I hear footsteps or a shuffling in the corner. On a number of occasions, I thought I heard a woman cry.'

'And have you investigated?'

'Yes, this house was once owned by the Chandler family. Fifty years ago, a young woman was betrothed to a soldier in Wellington's army.' Manning gazed quickly at Emma. 'Her fiancé was killed at Waterloo. The young woman never recovered. She became a recluse, locking herself away in this room. Tell me,' Manning continued, 'do you see anything?'

Grafeld shook his head. 'Not really. Just a feeling of deep depression, of sadness.'

'And what do you advise?'

'Your eminence, there are as many types of ghosts as there are human beings. I even hesitate to say the woman actually haunts the room. Perhaps it's just her desolation, so strong that it remains as a tangible, living thing, like breath on a frosty morning.'

'Should I ignore it?' Manning watched the young priest carefully. Over the years the Archbishop had interviewed many of the cranks and counterfeits who loved to dabble in religion, the so-called mystics who saw visions, the weak-minded and those who lived in a perpetual state of religious hysteria. Grafeld was none of these. He talked of the afterlife, of ghosts, haunting and exorcism as calmly and as coolly as another priest would collections on a Sunday or where to place a new pulpit. Manning made up his mind, Grafeld was the best choice. The priest was now staring round the room.

'What do you recommend, Father?'

'Has a Mass ever been said here?'

'Not to my knowledge.'

'Then I suggest you do. A simple low Mass offered for the repose of the soul of the Chandler woman. Once that is done, I'm sure you'll experience no further phenomena.'

'Is that why my brother was brought here?'

Emma had allowed the conversation to go over her head. She knew Oliver had gifts and was used to them. She had been with Oliver when Arthur had died. Anyone who had experienced what had happened afterwards would never be afraid again. Emma was eminently practical. Her brother could worry about souls; she worried about him. He was the son she would have liked to have, so naïve, he should never be allowed to wander round by himself. Others called this stupidity but Emma often wondered if Oliver had ever really grown up. Had something in him stopped after brother Arthur had died? Was Oliver still an innocent-eyed child with the body and inclinations of a man? If so, he should be treated gently and this Archbishop was getting on her nerves. He had asked a spate of questions, testing Oliver as if he were some charlatan.

'I'll tell you why both of you are here.' Manning beamed at her. 'But let me put it into perspective. The Catholic Church does not like talk of ghosts, demons or exorcisms. Indeed, it frowns upon them. That has always been the practice of our Church.' He plucked a letter from the file and held it delicately in his fingers, his eyes never leaving Oliver's. 'If this is true of the Church generally then even more so of the Catholic Church in England. It is only thirty-six years since it was allowed to exist legally in these islands. Only fifteen since Pius XI restored the hierarchy. Indeed, we are still in the catacombs. We are tolerated, sometimes respected but never liked. Our parishes can be divided into two: the working class, the majority of whom are immigrants from Ireland, Italy, Spain and elsewhere. On the other hand, the old English Catholics, aristocratic families who have supported the Church for generation after generation since the Reformation. I want you to help one of these.'

Manning cleared his throat. 'I have received a letter from Lady Alice Seaton. She is distantly related to the Howards, the Dukes of Norfolk. She owns a great house and estates just outside Norwich. She is about forty years of age, a good, kind woman, a loyal supporter of the Church. Three months ago Lady Alice's husband was killed in a riding accident. They had no children. Lady Alice lives at Candleton Hall with a retinue of servants. She is well known and respected for both her piety and kindness.' Manning forced a smile. 'She is my personal friend. About a month ago Lady Alice visited me in London.

She was calm and collected though I could sense her anxiety, a feeling of desperation. She described certain phenomena occurring at the Hall: a feeling of menace, of being watched, of seeing things. There had been noises at night, strange rappings and knockings, footsteps outside her bedroom.'

'She is of sound mind?' Oliver asked.

'As sound as you or I, Father.'

Oliver put his cup back on the table. 'But she is a widow?' he asked. 'Grieving?'

'What are you implying, Father? That her nerves are strained? That she is hallucinating?'

'Perhaps.'

Manning shook his head. 'Lady Alice is not like that.' He glanced quickly at Emma. 'Your sister reminds me a great deal of her. She's level-headed and keeps her imagination under control. She believes a great evil has entered her house. I would like you to go there, Father Oliver, you and your sister, to investigate. Do what is necessary.'

'There are two problems, your eminence,' Oliver replied quickly. 'And I must be honest with you. First, these phenomena could be the result of Lady Alice's state of mind. But I appreciate,' he added hastily, 'that you do not believe that. Nevertheless, if I am to go, this is not like Benfleet's house in Seven Dials. It could prove to be much more complex. Lady Alice will have to be honest with me.'

'And secondly?'

Oliver rubbed his chin. He just wished the Archbishop would not fence with him.

'If,' he replied slowly, 'Candleton is haunted and, if that presence or manifestation is evil, and I admit I am now contradicting myself, then there is a similarity between it and Benfleet's house in Seven Dials.'

'Are you implying that Lady Alice is guilty of some crime?'

'No, your eminence, I am saying it could be much more

dangerous. Evil can lie dormant. In eternity there is no time. Like seeds in the soil, evil can take root and, when it wishes, manifest itself. If that is the case, then my visit to Candleton may be more than a few hours and I might not be successful. Do you remember the parable from the gospels about the enemy sowing weeds amongst the wheat and Christ said that the weeds must not be pulled out lest the wheat came with it? That could apply to Candleton. The evil could be part of the fabric, like threads in a tapestry – pull one loose and rents will appear.'

'Lady Alice,' the Archbishop replied, 'will accept whatever help you can offer.' He opened a drawer and took out a brown manila envelope. 'I have booked seats for both of you on the Great Eastern Railway as well as two rooms at Jury's Hotel near Liverpool Street. Father Oliver, and you Miss Grafeld, I would appreciate it if you left for Norfolk tomorrow morning.' The Archbishop stood up and wagged an admonishing finger. 'Whatever happens must be kept secret!'

Matthew Bennington, a stone mason who lived on the outskirts of Candleton, finished his lunch of dark rye bread and cold ham. He stared around the chapel of St Edward the Confessor. The place was as silent as the grave. It stood some distance from Candleton Hall, shrouded by trees, and approached by a winding, pebbled path. The chapel, so local legend had it, was hundreds of years old with its long, narrow nave, soaring roof and pillars stretching up into the darkness. On the far side of these pillars ran gloomy transepts where the tombs of previous Seatons stood in forgotten grandeur.

'More like a morgue than a church,' Bennington mused aloud.

The benches had been cleared away. Even from where he sat on the altar steps looking through the rood screen, Bennington could see the range of coffin slabs which stretched down to the door of the church.

The mason was happy enough. He loved working with stone as his father had, and his father before him. He also felt privileged to be working in a place where, centuries earlier, other stone masons had laboured to prepare and dress the stone, leaving their own individual marks.

Bennington was working on a part of the wall behind the high altar which had begun to crumble due to damp. He was, admittedly, overawed by his surroundings. He attended local Quaker meetings and, although he would have nothing to do with popish ceremonies, he admired the high carved roof, the lovingly restored rood screen with its picture of Christ in the centre and, on either side, statues of St John and the Virgin Mary carved from dark polished wood. The windows were full of stained glass. Lady Alice had explained that these had been restored quite recently. Now the late-afternoon sun poured through in a glorious profusion of colours.

Bennington felt guilty at eating in such a hallowed place, yet it was so cold outside, and Lady Alice had been quite strict: he was not to leave the door open as the occasional fox or badger often wandered in to nestle in the warmth.

Bennington stared round the sanctuary. The altar stood behind him; to his right as he sat were the stalls, especially erected for the lord of the manor, to his left a large marble canopied tomb. Bennington had inspected that as soon as he entered the church.

'Built of Purbeck marble,' he had informed Lady Alice. 'This is not the work of some local craftsman.'

He'd crouched down and examined the armorial shields with their different colours, albeit faded, which decorated the rim of this tomb. He'd then brushed his hand along the carved Latin inscription on the side.

'Sir Henry Seaton,' Lady Alice explained. 'That's been there since 1486.'

She had knelt down beside the stone mason. Bennington

had liked that. Lady Alice was a strikingly good-looking woman much younger than her years, with her dark hair, pale skin and smiling green eyes. She wore a perfume the likes of which Bennington had never smelt before: rich and fragrant like flowers in a dell at the height of summer. She wasn't one to stand on ceremony, was Lady Alice.

'To my beloved husband.' She translated the Latin. 'Faithful unto death, who now rests with God, built by me his loving wife, Lady Isabella Seaton, December 1486. Three hundred and eighty years old,' Lady Alice added.

'She must have loved him,' Bennington observed.

'Oh, she did. And the tragedy is . . .' Lady Alice was going to continue her explanation when that interfering butler Maurice Stokes had waddled pompously into the church.

'Lady Alice! Lady Alice!' he had exclaimed. 'You are needed back at the house!'

'I'll explain later.' Lady Alice smiled. 'You must never ignore the butler.'

She had left, dress swirling. Bennington closed his eyes. If he could only catch that fragrance again. He would love to buy his wife something like that! How lovely to nestle up in a warm bed at night and have such fragrance tickle your nostrils.

'Why are you here?'

Bennington jumped. The words had been hissed. He got to his feet, feeling rather guilty about his thoughts of Lady Alice.

'Why are you here?' A woman's voice, angry, resentful.

'Is this a joke?' Bennington shouted, his words echoing through the empty church.

Bennington blamed his imagination and decided to return to work. He put the napkin in which the sandwiches had been wrapped in his haversack, collected his tools and went back to the stonework behind the altar. Bennington lit the three-branched candelabra Lady Alice had given him. He would work for another hour, perhaps an hour and a half, then when the clock struck four, he'd clean up and come back tomorrow. He grasped his chisel and wooden mallet and began to chip away at the rotting stone.

He closed his mind to everything and worked for about an hour. The light pouring through the large painted windows on either side of the sanctuary began to fade. Bennington still felt anxious, uneasy; picking up the candelabra, he walked round the altar and stared down the gloomy nave. Wisps of mist were seeping in under the door.

'Why are you here?' The whisper was hoarse, throaty.

Bennington whirled round. The voice came from the marble sarcophagus. As he moved the candle, Bennington noticed writing had appeared on the tomb, jagged, red as if someone had dipped their finger in paint and scrawled the words: 'What are you doing here?'

Bennington went over and crouched down. Was it blood? He got up and pinched his nostrils against the filthy smell. He caught a movement out of the corner of his eye and, glancing across the tomb, stared in horror at the figure hovering there. A woman, her dress black as night, a veil of the same colour wrapped around her scrawny throat. Her face was pallid as a corpse, the lips blood-red yet the eyes were only dark, sightless sockets.

Bennington screamed and dropped the candelabra. He ran down the church slithering and slipping. The spectre now stood, blocking the way out, the mist boiling around her. Bennington turned and a half-open door further down the church caught his attention. The crypt! He'd hide in the crypt!

Bennington ran. He knocked into one of the pillars but kept his balance and reached the door. As he rushed in, his heel missed the top step. The crypt steps were steep, their edges jagged. As Bennington fell, he glimpsed that hideous face glaring at him through the darkness. The pain was terrible. He couldn't stop himself falling. His head hit a sharp edge and, by the time his body reached the bottom, Bennington, stone mason from the village of Candleton, was dead.

At the far end of the cemetery, under the outstretched branches of a yew tree on which a faint coating of snow still dripped, Lady Alice Seaton stood with her personal maid, Ruth Brownlett, and stared down at her husband's grave.

The maid pulled her coat tightly round her. She was glad she was wearing a bonnet but she wished she'd brought the muffler as Cook had advised. It was not unknown for Lady Alice to stand for at least an hour over her husband's grave.

'She misses him terribly,' the cook had murmured. 'Sir Thomas was such a good man.'

Lady Alice looked over her shoulder and smiled. 'You can go in, Ruth – you're pinched with cold!'

'No, ma'am, I'd prefer to stay with you.'

'This is a good place,' Lady Alice observed. 'In a corner beneath a yew tree. My husband would have liked that.' She stared down at the white stone cross with its simple inscription: THE RIGHT HONOURABLE THOMAS SEATON, BART. 1817–1865 R.I.P.

Thomas had always fulminated against tearful epitaphs: he'd left strict instructions in his will that only his name, rank and years be given.

Lady Alice glanced across at the church. The door was shut. She really must go and check on Bennington yet she felt so weary. The occurrence of the previous night had frayed her nerves. Lady Alice was unwell but she dare not confide in anyone. She'd come round in her bedchamber, lying on the floor; when she had gone out into the gallery she had found nothing amiss.

'You've said your prayers, ma'am?'

Lady Alice walked back to join her maid. She tickled Ruth's nose with her gloved fingers.

'You are very good to come here. You need not.'

'Where madam goes, madam's maid always accompanies her,' Ruth replied.

Lady Alice gazed into the girl's clear brown eyes.

'You've noticed, haven't you?'

Ruth smiled cheekily. 'Ma'am, it's not every day the lady of the house asks her maid to sleep in the adjoining room. Ma'am, what is wrong? I know you still grieve but you are sick, restless. You should see Dr Meddlecott.'

'I will do. I will do.' Lady Alice's lips pursed into a thin line. 'I've talked to no one else, Ruth. I have sent for help from London. I expect guests tomorrow.'

'Help with what, ma'am?' Ruth's eyes fell away. 'I know,' she murmured. 'I've experienced it as well. Some of the servants are also beginning to whisper.'

'About what?'

'Dark shapes, ma'am; footsteps where no one walks; the rattling of doors, even singing . . .'

'Singing!' Lady Alice exclaimed.

'Yes, ma'am, a woman's voice, harsh. One of the chambermaids heard it, not English but French, a strange tune. A ghostly figure was seen in the Spanish Chamber looking at those pictures beneath the glass.'

'You mean the tapestry?'

'If you say so, ma'am.'

Lady Alice looked up at the darkening sky. She would not fuel rumours but nothing Ruth had said surprised her.

'And the servants know you study that painting!'

'Ah, Isabella!'

Ruth gazed back in puzzlement.

'Lady Isabella Seaton,' her mistress replied. 'She was lady of the manor during Tudor times. She erected that marble tomb in the chapel sanctuary.'

'If you say so, ma'am.'

Lady Alice chewed on the corner of her lip. She must

remember that Ruth, and many of the servants, were not Catholic and regarded the chapel as a strange place.

'They've also noticed strange things at the ruins,' Ruth explained. 'The old priory used to be where lovers met?'

Lady Alice nodded. She knew a great deal of the history of Seaton Hall. Across the great meadow, behind Foxley Copse, were the ruins of a small priory which had once been occupied by the Grey Friars. The monks had been turned out by Henry VIII's Commissioners at the Reformation.

'Are you saying ghosts are there as well?'

'So it's said, ma'am. A presence, strange sounds at night. Ma'am, it's freezing, we should go in.'

'You go back to the house,' Lady Alice replied. 'Tell Stokes I'll have tea in the parlour and remind Mrs Stokes that our guests will arrive, probably tomorrow afternoon or late in the evening. I'll need two guest rooms, on the same gallery as my chamber, cleaned and prepared.'

'The work has started, ma'am. Fires were lit to warm the rooms. Who are your guests, ma'am?'

'A Catholic priest, Father Grafeld, and his sister Miss Grafeld will be staying here for a while.'

'Are you sure I should leave you here, ma'am? It's growing dark.'

'Do not concern yourself, Ruth.'

Lady Alice watched her maid walk away. Ruth had been with her for six years. She trusted her but wondered how much the girl understood – if the other servants were talking the gossip would spread to the village.

Lady Alice crouched down by the grave and rearranged her small bouquet of white roses. The tumulus of earth which stood at the foot of the stone cross, protected by iron bars, had been freshly raked; the grass, still wet from the hoarfrost, clipped back.

He'd have insisted on that, Lady Alice reflected, always the one for order was Sir Thomas. Order in everything except his drinking! She wondered if Oliver Grafeld would help. Sir Thomas would have just laughed at her but were her dead husband and her feelings towards him the cause of all this? Was she being punished by God for her terrible sin?

She got to her feet and brushed the wet grass from her coat. Lady Alice pressed her hand against the twinge in her stomach. She really would have to have a long chat with Dr Meddlecott and, perhaps, Ralph? Lady Alice turned away, as if she wanted to hide her face from her husband's grave.

Lord Ralph Mowbray was a bachelor and a Catholic. Lady Alice had fallen in love with him as soon as they first met, just after she had returned from her honeymoon. Her marriage to Sir Thomas had been one of convenience, arranged by their parents. Lady Alice always thought her feelings for Ralph would disappear but, over the years, they had grown. She suspected that Lord Mowbray, despite his dapper looks and officer-trained manners, felt the same. Just a glance, now and again when their hands would brush at the different balls and parties; he would ask her for a dance and they'd swirl round the ballroom. Oh, they'd talked about crops, servants, the doings of Lord Russell, Palmerston or the arrogance of that popinjay Disraeli. Lord Mowbray, with his military bearing and staring blue eyes, that luxuriant moustache he always cultivated, was a shy man who would never speak to Alice unless she spoke first.

Never once, over the years, had either of them given Sir Thomas cause for suspicion. Not that he'd mind! Thomas had his own pursuits. Alice had heard the rumours about a young lady who lived in comfortable rooms in Norwich and there were chambermaids who came and went. But how could she reproach Thomas when he could so readily reproach her? Twenty years married and she'd never produced a healthy male heir. Nothing but sickly children who'd die within a month or miscarriages which had left her exhausted and depleted.

Now Lady Alice felt like crouching at the foot of a tree either laughing or crying at the unkindness of fate. She looked up and realised she had been walking aimlessly. She made her way along the path to the lych gate, out of the cemetery and down to the mere. The trees were silent. Now and again a bird would soar up above them into the icy blue sky. As the mist seeped over the grass, she glimpsed a small shape as a rabbit darted from the undergrowth.

'I wish winter would pass,' Alice whispered. It would be so lovely to feel the sun and hear the birds sing like choirs from the trees. It was hard to realise that she was now mistress of this place, that she had already made plans of her own. Again she felt a pain in her stomach, a feeling of nausea. Lady Alice paused to catch her breath; she must be careful.

She reached the reed-fringed mere and stared out across the water. In spring and summer this was a beautiful place. The sun would shimmer on the water while the different birds which nested there provided a wild profusion of colour and sound.

Lady Alice remembered how she and her husband used to walk down here before life turned sour and the reproaches began. The mere now suited her mood. The mist-hung water was still and as grey as steel.

Lady Alice was about to walk on when the sound of a horse, galloping fast and furious, shattered the silence. The pounding hoofbeats meant this was no pleasure ride or even a horse being exercised, yet its rider must be charging across the parkland! No one would ride where there was no path and the trees and dips in the ground made it highly dangerous. Lady Alice recalled old maps of Candleton. Hadn't there once been a trackway across here before it had been grassed over? The hoofbeats grew nearer, more insistent. Lady Alice stopped. The rider was approaching her, the jingle of harness, the snorting of a horse exhausted after a gruelling ride were quite distinct. Then it was gone, silence, as if it had never happened. A crow from one of the trees cawed raucously, a sharp crack in the ominous silence.

Lady Alice returned to the mere. Had someone poled the skiff out? The mist parted. Her fingers flew to her lips. A figure was moving across the mere towards her: hooded, caped, the face hidden behind a veil. Lady Alice stepped back but the figure glided closer.

'Lady Alice! Lady Alice!'

She whirled round. Dr Meddlecott was running down the hill. He reached her, huffing and puffing, his eyes bright, his boyish face flushed from the exertion. The top hat he sometimes wore, more for affectation than for dress, was clasped in his hand, his brown curly hair windswept and dishevelled.

'Whoops!' He steadied himself with his cane. 'Lady Alice, what are you doing in this freezing weather, standing by a lake staring into the mist? Lord, woman!' Meddlecott would never allow the dignity of status to blunt his speech. He grasped her hand and felt her face. 'You are freezing!' Meddlecott's concern deepened. Lady Alice was white as a sheet; her eyes had a glazed look as if on the verge of a faint. He put his arm round her shoulder, turning her back towards the Hall.

'No, no,' she muttered. 'I must see Bennington in the church.' She glanced up at him. 'He's a stone mason, he's . . .'

'You come back to the Hall. I'll see to Bennington.'

She broke free of his embrace and stepped away.

'William, did you see anything?'

'Yes, some grass, trees, a lake, mist and a moonstruck woman.'

Lady Alice glanced over her shoulder but the lake was empty, the ghastly figure was gone.

'And there's no horse rider approaching the Hall?'

'Lady Alice, what is the matter? No one would gallop across the park, certainly not in this weather!' He grasped her wrist.

'I'm your physician and you are coming back to the Hall where you'll tell me what this is all about.'

She resisted his pull. 'I don't think you'll believe me!'

'Oh, I can believe in ghosts.'

'No, no, William, it's not just that, I also think I'm with child.'

Chapter 4

Father Oliver Grafeld fell in love with Candleton as soon as he glimpsed its towers, turrets and chimney stacks when the two-horse-drawn carriage broke from the trees and followed the winding lane around to the main gateway. He leaned back against the cushioned seat and nudged his sister.

'Come on, Emma, it's not the end of the world. Better here than Seven Dials!'

Emma refused to look at him. She grinned mischievously and pulled up the woollen rug.

They had left London on their first-class tickets early that morning. Emma was much taken by the carriage, the steam engine and the speed whereby they cut through the countryside though both she and Oliver were rather shaken and cold by the time they reached Norwich. Thompson, who now sat on the seat before them, cracking his whip over the two grey mares, had grabbed their luggage and secured it on the back, introducing himself while he did so.

'Lady Alice sent me,' he announced in a sing-song voice. 'Told me to take the open carriage.' He pointed up at the sky. 'The day is fine.' He gave a leery grin. 'The springs on this be much better than the old one.'

They had stopped at a wayside inn for some breakfast served from the buffet: sausage, eggs, thick wedges of fried bread and steaming mugs of strong, sweet tea. Thompson chattered like a magpie for the rest of the journey, about how there were few visitors to Candleton so they'd be made most welcome. As he cracked his whip, Oliver had noticed how Thompson occasionally helped himself from a little hip flask and he just prayed the old man, who now and again swayed dangerously on the seat, didn't fall asleep and tumble off.

'Whoa there! Whoa!'

Oliver started. Looking round Thompson, he saw a horse and cart approaching them. Thompson skilfully manoeuvred the carriage to the side of the lane without letting the wheels fall into the ditch. The dray horse pulling the wooden cart came on. Its driver exchanged greetings with Thompson.

'In the funeral business now I am!' he called.

Oliver and Emma watched the cart trundle by, the coffin slung in the back bouncing and moving the rough-hewn cross nailed on its lid. Oliver muttered a requiem and crossed himself. Emma did likewise.

'That's poor old Bennington,' Thompson remarked. 'Took a fall down the crypt steps he did: dead as a door nail! The mistress and Dr Meddlecott found him there last night. Poor bugger, I hope he wasn't drinking.' He turned an unshaven cheek and grinned. 'Drink can be a terrible curse!'

Thompson studied these two strangers closely. Both dressed in black, they looked tidy and neat but rather shabby, as were their cases.

'You're the popish priest, are you not?'

'I am a priest,' Oliver replied.

Thompson was sharp enough to catch the distaste on Emma's face. A little virago there, he thought. His face creased in apology.

'I'm sorry, Father, that's what Lady Alice told me to call you, "Father Oliver". It sounds better than vicar, don't you agree?' He cracked his whip and continued.

Emma and Oliver stared across the misty parkland, a broad green expanse, dotted with clumps of trees, which sloped up towards the Hall. Emma exclaimed in surprise as a roe deer burst out from behind one of the trees and daintily trotted across, its hooves hardly seeming to touch the ground. Her gaze took in the house, the moat, the great red-bricked walls, the mullioned glass windows reflecting the weak sunlight, the black slate roof, the flag bearing the Seaton arms, an eagle with its wings outstretched.

'It's like something from a fairy story!' she exclaimed.

'Aye, that it is,' the irrepressible Thompson agreed. 'A happy place, Candleton. The mistress is a good lord. Mind you, so was Sir Thomas in his day.'

'In his day?' Oliver sat forward.

'He was a good man, a kind manor lord but he liked his drink, did Sir Thomas, as well as his horses and dogs. Lady Alice has given them to a neighbour on loan. The Candleton hunt has moved house for a while. Well, we shall soon be there.'

Thompson cracked his whip, the horses trotted a little faster. The carriage spun up through the gates and along the broad thoroughfare leading to the bridge across the moat dominated by a massive gatehouse.

'Lady Isabella Seaton built that,' Oliver told his sister. 'As she did most of the Hall. A great Tudor lady, she was born in the reign of Henry VI and lived to see Henry VIII dissolve the monasteries. They say she loved Candleton more than she did her own soul or the joys of Heaven.'

'I can see why,' Emma said. 'But, Oliver, I still object to what the Archbishop did. You are a priest and an exorcist, not some freak in a county fair!'

'The Archbishop was testing me,' Oliver retorted. 'His eminence is like that. He has to be careful.'

'Did you ever find out what happened at Seven Dials?' Emma asked.

The beauty of Candleton was such a sharp contrast to the mean streets and shabby houses of that squalid place, Oliver wondered if it was all a nightmare. He shuddered as he recalled that cellar full of stinking corpses.

'Well?' Emma insisted.

'I advised it should be cleaned, painted and blessed.' Oliver pushed back his broad-brimmed hat and scratched his forehead. 'Or, better still, razed to the ground. Thank God we are not there now, eh, sister?'

The carriage rattled over the stone bridge. Oliver gazed to his right. The reed-filled moat looked pleasant and he glimpsed ripples from the carp and tench which swam there. Across the hill, further to his left, he glimpsed the spire of the manor church rising above the tall yew trees and the black stone wall which surrounded the cemetery. Oliver had done his homework well, being in possession of a copy of *The Manor Houses of Old England*. Candleton Hall had figured prominently in it.

They went through under the yawning gatehouse. The arch itself was vaulted and stone-ribbed; on each corner the heads of gargoyles leered down at him. Then they were through into the main gravel-lined courtyard. Ostlers and grooms came forward. Oliver gazed appreciatively round.

'It's built like many others.' He couldn't resist giving his sister a lecture. 'That will be the main hall with galleries above; two wings have been added while the gatehouse line contains the stables and outhouses.'

'Oliver, for goodness' sake!' Emma hissed. 'Our host . . .'

The priest hurriedly stepped down from the carriage. Across the courtyard the main door stood open. A woman dressed in a black silk dress, a cape of the same colour over her shoulders, came out towards them. An attractive woman, Oliver thought. The thin face was pale but the eyes were beautiful, the mouth smiling, her rich black hair sprinkled with grey. At first glance she looked middle-aged but closer she seemed young, even youthful. She stretched out a hand sheathed in a black laced mitten.

'Father Oliver, Miss Grafeld, you are most welcome to Candleton.'

Oliver remembered his manners quickly enough to raise the

hand to his lips and kiss it. Lady Alice then embraced Emma, hugging her close.

'I'm so glad you've both come.' Lady Alice stepped back, eyes bright. 'Was your journey comfortable?'

Too tense, Oliver thought. Lady Alice was a tall, graceful woman with a beautiful face but, try as she might, she couldn't hide her anxiety. She found it difficult to stand still, her gaze moving constantly from him to Emma and then beyond to where the ostlers were unhitching the horses.

'Come in! Come in!'

She waved them in through the porchway and into the hall. A youngish man stepped forward. He was dressed in a grey suit with a burgundy-coloured waistcoat; a cravat of the same colour was held in place by a diamond stud. The starched, high-winged collar supported a fleshy chin.

'Dr William Meddlecott,' Lady Alice said.

The doctor grasped Oliver's hand, squeezing it so tightly Oliver winced: Meddlecott's weather-beaten face broke into a smile.

'I am sorry, I am sorry, Father, my grip is too strong.' But his merry brown eyes had already left the priest, he seemed fascinated by Emma. 'Madam, you must be Father Oliver's sister?' He abruptly became rather withdrawn.

'I am certainly not his wife!' Emma retorted.

The doctor blushed in embarrassment. Most women he met were coy and simpering but Emma actually drew closer, studying him closely.

'You look well after your journey,' he stammered.

'They are tired,' Lady Alice said. 'Stokes!'

The portly butler, swinging his arms like a soldier on parade, walked forward, a picture of rectitude in his black tailed suit and spotless white shirt, a striped waistcoat with a fob watch decorating his broad front. He looked portly and, Emma thought, slightly ridiculous; she had to bite her lips to stop laughing. The butler, hands now hanging at his sides, bowed stiffly to her and then to Oliver.

'Madam, shall I show them to their rooms?'

'No, no, Stokes. I'll show them up. Tell the porters and Thompson to bring the luggage up later. Come, Father, you and Emma are both on the same gallery as myself.'

Lady Alice led them up the broad staircase. She gripped the shiny, open balustrade, pressing a little too hard. Oliver sensed Lady Alice was not well, but he chattered about the weather, the journey and the Great Eastern Railway. Lady Alice asked about Archbishop Manning and would the Pope create him a Cardinal? Was London any cleaner? Then how Father Oliver and Emma were not to worry about anything, they were her guests.

Oliver half-listened. The staircase was beautiful with its thick carpet down the centre, the intricately carved newels works of art. Along the walls hung numerous oil paintings, but Oliver ignored these as he tried to imagine the house as a medieval manor. The gallery Lady Alice led them along was dark, lined with pictures and small tables covered in artefacts. The paper on the walls showed a silver fleur de lys on a light-blue background. The bedchamber Lady Alice showed them into was just as tastefully decorated: a table in front of the window, high-backed, quilted chairs, a large china bowl and jug on the dresser, wardrobes and a small four-poster bed draped in blue and gold curtains.

'There's no gas I am afraid,' Lady Alice explained. She gestured at the large candelabra which stood around the room and the brass oil lamps on the table. 'But there's enough light.' She pointed to the bell rope in the corner. 'And, if you want anything, day or night, just ring. Stokes is ever so attentive. Come on, Emma, I'll show you your bedroom.'

Oliver was pleased to close the door behind them. He sat on the bed and took out his breviary. Lady Alice had thought of everything. Against the far wall was a prie-dieu beneath a crucifix. He went across and knelt to read that part of the divine office he had been unable to finish on his journey. There was a knock on the door; Stokes and others brought in his luggage which they placed at the foot of the bed.

'We'll unpack for you, sir.'

'Yes, later, everything except the valise. It has personal possessions.'

'You didn't bring vestments did you, sir?' Stokes looked disapprovingly at him. 'Lady Alice has a set of her own in the chapel sacristry.'

'No, no, I didn't. That's very thoughtful of Lady Alice.'

Stokes bowed and left. Oliver finished his reading and sat in one of the armchairs placed so he could look out of the window over the park. He heard sounds from the gallery; Emma's faint laughter from next door, Dr Meddlecott's gruff tones. Oliver smiled to himself. Emma had made another conquest. The priest reflected on what Manning had hinted at, but what could he do? He loved Emma and his sister, six years his senior, was so insistent.

She had lost her husband in the troubles in India. They had no other family so Emma, who had always been so protective about him, even throughout her married life, had simply arrived and stayed. In many ways she was a good companion, sharp, incisive, practical with a ready sense of humour. Beneath her brittle exterior, Emma was calm and patient. She took each day as it came and accepted her brother's calling to be a priest and his duties as an exorcist as part of everyday life. The only problem was that she was both very pretty and looked younger than her years. There had been gossip, sniggers behind raised hands until people realised that Emma was Oliver's sister and the relationship was no source of scandal. Oliver recalled Manning's shrewd eyes.

'Is that another reason why I'm an exorcist?' he murmured.

'My Church is only too willing to move me from parish to parish.'

Oliver stared out of the window. It had been a fine day, the sun strong enough to burn the hoarfrost, but now it was beginning to dip, making the trees look black and stark. Another rap on the door: a chambermaid bustled in carrying a heavy coal scuttle. Oliver offered to help but she shook her head. She built up the fire, neatly swept the hearth and left as quietly as she came.

Oliver stared round the room. It was strange, when he went to houses, such as Benfleet's in Seven Dials, he had always felt a presence but there was nothing here, only Lady Alice tense and eager to please. Was he wasting his time?

'Father Oliver?'

Lady Alice stood in the doorway.

'I am sorry,' she said. 'Didn't you hear me knock?'

He rose. 'No, no, my lady . . .'

'Oh stop that, Alice is my name.' She sat on a chair opposite. 'I'm glad you've arrived. Father Oliver, Dr Meddlecott is showing your sister round the house now. If you like, I will take you.'

Oliver agreed. 'But,' he added, 'I would prefer if you do not tell me anything. Let me receive my own impressions.'

'Will you say Mass for us tonight, Father, before dinner? There'll only be four of us; Dr Meddlecott, myself, you and Miss Grafeld. We can talk then.'

Oliver agreed and Lady Alice took him on a tour of Candleton Hall.

Oliver soon became aware of the Hall's rich and varied history. In the downstairs salon Pugin had worked to create its gothic windows; the red flocked wallpaper, devised by the decorator J.G. Grace from a design by Pugin, harmonised with the colours of the great frieze above the marble mantelpiece. Delicate furniture stood on carpets from England, Turkey and

India. Large buffets; costly china plate; shelf after shelf of books which made Oliver's fingers positively itch to take them down. There were busts and portraits of former Seatons and royal charters, tastefully framed in ebony wood, the glass highlighting the black medieval script.

In the old drawing room display cabinets contained miniatures, jewellery, enamels and family memorabilia. The library, with its flock gilt wallpaper, possessed a very decorative carpet manifesting the Seaton heraldic devices in red and gold as well as a handsome Tudor fireplace with a carved over-mantel, which displayed the arms of the Seatons and the different families they had married into. In the hallway stood a long case clock and ornate rosewood stools. Leading off that was the small dining room with its exuberant designs, Belgian cabinets, tables and chairs.

Lady Alice took him through the stone-flagged kitchens, buttery and bakery, a hive of activity, the air full of fragrant smells which made the priest's mouth water. She noticed the expression on his face and her fingers flew to her lips.

'I have offered you no refreshment! Good Lord, Father, what kind of a hostess am I?' She became quite agitated. 'I am very sorry, very sorry!'

They returned to the small drawing room where Stokes served tea, scones, cream and jam. All the time Lady Alice chattered, telling Oliver about the different incidents from Candleton's history: the rogues and heroes, saints and scholars, traitors and Kings' Councillors who had lorded it here since the Conqueror's time. It was a chequered family history for the Seatons, unlike many noble families, had adhered to Rome. Despite heavy fines and impositions, they had remained loyal to the faith even during the most fierce persecution.

'There are secret rooms here,' Lady Alice laughingly explained as they began their tour again. 'But they are so secret no one can find them.'

She led Oliver back up the stairs along the different floors. They passed Emma and Dr Meddlecott deep in conversation in a window seat at the end of one gallery.

'I am fascinated by your sister's experiences as a nurse,' Dr Meddlecott called out.

'No he's not,' Emma laughed back. 'He's only flattering me.'

Lady Alice, grasping Oliver by the wrist, simply waved at them and passed on.

Oliver grew ever more aware of the Hall which had stood and developed since the eleventh century. Different pieces had been added on according to the fortunes of the Seaton family. As they left by the east staircase, Lady Alice walked rather quickly by one room, its door set back in a recess. The portal itself was of gothic design, the wood unlike the rest, being a dark mahogany with metal studs. Oliver glanced at it quickly: the wood must be at least four hundred years old. Only there did he experience a feeling of unease. However, Lady Alice was so insistent on showing him the King's Room on the bottom floor of the east end of the manor that he did not stop to question her.

The King's Room was spacious, with a large brick fireplace and moulded beams in the ceiling. Lady Alice explained how the oak linen-fold panelling round the walls was of an exquisite Belgian design; the furniture here was heavy, the glass in the window, like that of a church, painted in various hues. Oliver judged it must date back at least to the sixteenth century.

'It's called the King's Chamber,' Lady Alice explained. 'Because Henry VII stayed here on his royal tour of the eastern counties in 1503. He was much taken by the Hall and its occupants and left them all the richer. Come, I shall show you the garden.'

This lay behind the Hall. It was laid out in the French parterre style, each section edged with cotton, lavender and small boxwood hedges. There was a kitchen garden, herbal plots, and two squares of plum and greengages with quinces at the corners. A mixture of climbing roses, clematis and young sweetsbane rambled along the walls. At the far end was an old peach house and, beyond that, a small orchard of apple and pear trees.

A beautiful place, Oliver considered, even on this cold December day.

'In summer it attracts the sun,' Lady Alice explained. 'I'll show you the grounds, or would you rather explore them yourself?'

'Yes, I'd like to ride round. I'll see the chapel tonight when I say Mass.'

'There is one other place,' Lady Alice went on, her eyes not meeting his. 'I think you realise that, don't you Father?'

'I saw the door,' Oliver admitted.

She took him back to the east wing. They climbed the stairs to the chamber. Lady Alice opened a small purse which hung at the waist of her dress, took out a silver key and unlocked the door. Oliver stepped inside.

A narrow gothic window in the far wall provided enough light to see clearly. The ceiling was of heavy timbers but every inch of the walls was covered in thick blood-red Spanish leather, which gave the room a sombre appeal. The floor also was covered in the same material though centuries' use had left it marked and scuffed. There was no furniture except for a table and chair beneath the window.

'I've never seen anything like this!'

'I have,' Lady Alice exclaimed, closing the door behind them. She picked up the box of matches from the table and lit the candelabra. 'Such rooms are common in Spanish palaces. They called them secret chambers.'

'Yes, I can see why.'

The leather covering everywhere conjured up a place where conspirators could gather and whisper secrets, knowing there were no eyelets or peep-holes in the walls. Oliver examined the leather. It felt at least five or six inches thick and, although faded, bore a decorative motif of red and white roses.

'What do you call this room?' Oliver took out his spectacles and put them on.

'The Spanish Chamber or Lady Isabella's room.'

'Ah yes. She was lady of the manor for a considerable time during the Tudor period.'

'This is her portrait.'

Oliver turned. On that part of the wall to the right of the doorway hung a small, square painting; next to it, a large piece of glass protected a broad, colourful tapestry. He noticed that Lady Alice was not so friendly now. She went and stood next to the window, as if the fading sunlight afforded some protection.

Oliver walked across. The heavy floor covering deadened any sound and heightened the sense of being in a dream, cut off from the rest of the house. He stared at the painting which was done in oils by someone who had tried to imitate the great court painters of the Tudor period. It was more a stereotype than a portrait, as instanced by the ornate Tudor head veil and black dress with a collar. Oliver scrutinised the face framed by the veil. He blinked and looked again, holding his spectacles steady on his nose. The more he did, the more he realised the artist had caught something intangible in those staring eyes and determined mouth.

He fetched the candelabra from the table and returned to his scrutiny. The face in the painting was well proportioned, the skin fashionably white, the nose straight but the head was slightly turned away. The more Oliver stared the more certain he became that the face was sneering, exuding a malevolence as well as the arrogance of a woman of high birth and great power. She gave the impression of holding many secrets but did not see why she should share these with the world at large.

He read the inscription on the gilt frame: Lady Isabella Seaton 1465 to 1554.

'A long life,' Oliver whispered.

He repressed a shiver. Suddenly he whirled round; Lady Alice was standing behind, staring at him. Oliver narrowed his eyes over the top of his spectacles. Something else was here: a presence, an echo, unsavoury and unpleasant.

'The tapestry, Father, have a look at that.'

Oliver, holding the candle, studied the tapestry protected by its huge piece of glass. At first he thought it was a hunting frieze. He could see the trees, horsemen, dogs, a deer, but the closer he studied, the more his disquiet grew. Other scenes were woven in – a small army in one corner, knights in armour holding lances advancing under furling banners. A little way across stood a clump of trees where a corpse dangled. The other scenes were wild glimpses from a nightmare: a man pierced by an arrow and tied to a pole carried by a duck-billed devil. A club-footed monster with a hamper full of souls strapped to his back. A pimply, spongy-bellied devil turning a spit on which a man was lashed. Demons hissed as they danced round the fire; devils flew up against a blood-filled sun. Further down the tapestry was a broken-down house peopled by demons with bat wings and goats' heads.

Oliver stared in disbelief. The tapestry was very old and some of the colours were faded but the vivid scenes were the work of a tormented soul. He almost forgot the atmosphere in the room as he edged along the tapestry which was at least four feet high and eight across.

'It's exquisite needlework!' he exclaimed.

'The work of Mathilda Seaton,' Lady Alice explained. 'She was the daughter of Isabella's first husband, Sir Henry. They say she was fey, mad: that tapestry was the work of many years.'

Oliver stared down at the right-hand corner and made out the words *Mathilda me fecit, Mathilda made me, Anno Domini 1555*.

'The poor girl lived here. Of course, no one would take her

in marriage. She died a recluse a year after Lady Isabella and lies buried in the crypt beneath the church.' Lady Alice paused. 'You feel uncomfortable, don't you, Father?'

Oliver nodded. 'It could just be a darkened chamber. Perhaps it still retains memories, an aura. Like perfume, when it is spilt on the floor, the stain can disappear but the fragrance remains. It is strange, when I first came in here, I was excited by a truly gothic chamber, redolent of the Middle Ages; dark leather coverings on the walls, little furniture, the oak-beamed ceiling, the metal-studded door.'

'I felt the same,' Lady Alice said. 'At first, it's welcoming, strange, rather exotic but the more you stay, the more uncomfortable it becomes. Now, Father . . .'

She took him down to the stables where one of the ostlers saddled a gentle-looking grey cob. Oliver confessed he was a poor horseman but he had ridden a similar type of mount as he worked among the villages of South Essex. He politely refused Lady Alice's offer to accompany him and eased himself up into the saddle.

'Just follow the paths, Father.' She looked up at the darkening sky. 'But don't be too long.'

Oliver dug his heels in and the old cob moved forward, head down, at a leisurely pace over the bridge. At first Oliver had some difficulties with the reins but the cob was docile and friendly and the priest soon settled down to an enjoyable ride.

The sun was setting, the shadows lengthening; overhead, crows cawed raucously at the fading daylight. Rabbits scampered along the grass. A roe deer burst out of a thicket, head turned: it watched Oliver for a while and then galloped furiously back. Now and again the priest passed servants coming to and from the Hall, cheerful people who raised their hands in salutation.

Oliver let the cob find its way across the grass and down to the mere. The lake was peaceful with a small, overgrown island in the centre. An occasional bird skimmed across the water while, among the reeds, a warbler sang its last song of the day.

Oliver turned his horse towards the church, the old ruins of Greyfriars, the orchards and the out gardens, always keeping the house in full view. He did not want to embarrass either himself or his hostess by becoming lost.

He took his fob watch out. It was almost five o'clock and soon it would be dark. He turned the cob up a small gravel path which wound past the church back towards the house. As he rounded a corner, the cob abruptly started.

A man stood in the centre of the pathway, staring wild-eyed at Father Oliver. He was dressed in a knee-length robe, leggings beneath pushed into boots on which spurs clinked. He carried a dagger in his hand, his hair was long and framed a pallid, youthful face. The cob reared and the priest fought hard to keep his seat; when he looked again, the man had vanished.

Oliver tried to see where he had gone. Everything was silent. He leant down and patted his horse's neck. The man had been dressed in medieval garb. Oliver realised it could not be a joke so it must have been a ghost, a phantasm. He whispered reassuringly to the horse, gathered the reins and made his way slowly along the path which led up to the bridge, across the moat and back into the courtyard.

Under the cavernous gateway Oliver turned his horse. He stared back across the bridge along the winding path. He was about to dismount when he glimpsed the shadow, dark and ominous, under the outstretched branch of one of the great oak trees.

'*Jesus misere!*' Oliver whispered. He took a deep breath to ease his shock and panic. 'You've eluded me so far,' he went on. 'Now you boldly show yourself.'

Oliver had no doubts about what that dark shape represented. It looked like the outline of a woman heavily veiled and cloaked. He sensed the menace, the commitment to evil that figure embodied. It stood there, motionless, like a plume of black smoke coughed up by Hell. It did not move or waver and, although the face was hidden, Oliver realised that its hateful stare had made him turn. He wanted to stand his ground until it disappeared but he recalled his training, that would be a childish contest of wills, not the duty of an exorcist. He dismounted and gave the reins to an ostler.

'Is there anything wrong, Father?'

The priest smiled. 'No, lad, nothing that won't wait.'

Oliver took off his coat and hat. He stopped to ease the cramp in his thighs and went in by a side door. After taking directions from a maid, he walked round, up the main staircase to his own bedchamber. As he sat down to take off his boots, Emma knocked at the door and came in.

'Before you ask,' Oliver declared, 'there is a Presence here, Emma. Very sinister, very strong!'

Chapter 5

The Presence, as Father Oliver described it, had now moved to the top of a hill and surveyed the valley which separated it from Candleton Hall. The Presence had a consciousness and will all of its own, a brooding awareness of its power and intent. In its perception, the sky above Candleton's blue-grey walls was a reddish-orange while the world in which it lived was full of eerie images and visions. A three-dimensional view of reality, an accumulation of what had been, what is and what might be. The Presence was aware of evening time, of the birds' hushed song, of the Hall and the people within it.

Over the centuries its will, its commitment to evil had grown and strengthened. Now it believed its time had come again. In the chaos of its own private Hell, everyday objects had swollen to monstrous proportions, reflections of a nightmare, scraps and fragments of its own dark soul. In its vision of Hell, a corpse was attached by two devils to the branches of a leprous white tree; another was helplessly entangled in blood-soaked undergrowth while a third was drowned in the freezing waters of the lake. Strange birds filled the sky. Armies moved across a blood-soaked plain, lancers levelled, shields prepared. A demon-faced rabbit chased a fox. The air was full of screams and strange cries. A figure crossed its path, dressed garishly in a tawdry yellow dress, the swollen face shrouded by a red kerchief.

The Presence ignored all these, conscious only of the Hall, of the evil it had done and the evil it would continue to wreak.

The Presence was not afraid of the priest or the power he represented. The Presence had always lived in its own world, refusing good in life and so refusing it in death. Its memories, as well as the memories of all those earth-bound around it, made up its reality. Demons, dark shapes and shadows, came and went. The Presence's own experiences of life were vividly present. Men in armour riding out to battle, the blue-gold banner, with the spread eagle of the Seatons, flapping bravely against the garish sky. Whispered conversations, secrets hatched hundreds of years ago, still echoed like a bell through a lonely churchyard. Armies rushed against each other; a wolf attacked a man on a desolate road; a group of executioners hoisted a man over the branch of a tree and laughed and jeered at the way their victim's legs danced and his face grew grotesque as he gasped for air; another man sat on the bridge, a knife in his ribs; several dogs with slavering jaws ran up to tear at his flesh.

The Presence hovered. Invisible to the eye, it summoned up its own conscious strength. Candleton Hall was still the centre and focus of its life, as it had been hundreds of years ago when its will and the intellect, encumbered by the flesh, had plotted murder, treachery and deceit in order to possess the place to its fullness. The Presence constantly raged against the darkness around it, seeking a way out, a fresh place to inhabit: it now believed it had found this.

The Presence gathered itself up, moving down towards the Hall, eager to repossess what it considered its own. The doomed soul was full of its own certainties. It had never asked for a pardon or compassion and, for all eternity, never would.

'*Ite Missa est*.' Father Oliver made the sign of the cross, stooped and kissed the sanctuary stone. He then turned and walked down the altar steps.

'Thank you, Father.'

Lady Seaton came out of her stall on the other side of the sanctuary. She, Dr Meddlecott and Emma joined the priest in the sacristy and helped him to divest as well as clear the altar.

'A jewel of a chapel,' Father Oliver observed.

He stared appreciatively around; with its wooden panelling, fitted cupboards and shelves, the sacristy was well ordered and stocked. In a glass case on the far wall stood chalices and patens dating back centuries.

'Mass has always been said here,' Lady Alice said proudly. 'Ever since the Hall was founded.' She pointed to a board displaying a list of names near the sacristy door. 'Since the first chapel was built in 1101 there have been one hundred and ninety-five chaplains.' She pulled a face. 'Though the post is presently vacant. Father Ferreby died a year ago. We petitioned the Vicar General but priests are few and far between in Norfolk.' She stared at Father Oliver as if hoping the priest would make some offer. 'Ah well,' she said busily. 'I'll show you the rest of the church.'

They went back into the sanctuary. Father Oliver looked to his right through the rood screen down to the main door. He glimpsed it, a shadow deeper than the rest, but decided to ignore it.

Lady Alice, who seemed much calmer, took them round the church. She showed them the Lady Chapel and the chantry of St Edward the Confessor as well as the different memorial slabs and the gravestones down the nave. During the Mass Father Oliver had been taken by the great tomb on the right side of the sanctuary.

'Of pure Purbeck marble,' Lady Alice told him. 'It's not really a tomb. More of a memorial. You see, Sir Henry Seaton was a widower. In 1482, he married a local girl, Isabella Bruton: he was a good twenty years her senior yet it appeared to have been a love match. Now, in 1483, Edward IV died. Richard III usurped the throne. In the summer of 1485, Henry Tudor landed in South Wales and made his bid for the throne . . .'

'You should have been a school teacher,' Dr Meddlecott murmured.

'Hush!' Lady Alice teased him back. 'This is one of the most exciting parts of the Hall's history and I'll have my say.'

She went and stood by the priest who had crouched down to read the inscription on the side of the sarcophagus.

'The Seatons,' she continued, 'had always supported the House of York. So, despite King Richard having a wicked reputation, Sir Henry decided to throw in his lot with him. However, he decided to hedge his bets. Sir Henry had two grown sons from his previous marriage, Ralph and Benedict: Ralph would go and fight for the Tudor alongside a distant kinsman of Sir Henry's, a man called Lord Montague, while Henry and Benedict declared for Richard.'

'Can you follow all this?' Dr Meddlecott winked at Emma.

'Most closely,' Oliver quipped back. ' "An honest tale speaks best to be plainly told." Scene one, Act Four, *Richard III*,' he added, seeing the puzzlement on Meddlecott's face. 'What happened next, Lady Alice?'

'A tragedy. As you know, Richard III was defeated at Bosworth. Ralph, fighting strenuously for Henry Tudor, was killed in the battle.'

'And Sir Henry and Benedict?' Emma asked.

'Ralph's death was a tragedy,' Lady Alice said. 'But Henry, well, he was murdered. Oh, he was given a mock trial but, in those few hours after the battle, when the blood still ran hot, Sir Henry was accused of being the most ardent supporter of the usurper and hanged out of hand.'

'Yes, yes, that's so,' Oliver agreed. 'Even before the battle threats had been made to Richard's followers, including John Howard, Duke of Norfolk. How did the note go? Ah yes! "Jockey of Norfolk, ride not so bold, for Dickon your master has been bought and sold." I have studied Polydor Virgil's account of the battle. He was an Italian who came to England during Henry's reign. A number of Richard's followers suffered such a fate, including Sir William Catesby.'

'What happened to Sir Henry's corpse?' Emma asked.

'According to the accounts, Henry Tudor, now styling himself Henry VII, ordered its release and transport back here. The corpse never arrived. For years afterwards Lady Isabella petitioned the King's Council for redress. She was heartbroken and so this memorial was erected here in the sanctuary. Even the King was shamefaced and made a contribution towards it, as did others of his Council, including the Earls of Pembroke and Oxford.'

'What happened to Benedict Seaton?' Meddlecott asked.

'He just disappeared, no sign, no trace of him after Bosworth.'

'And Lady Isabella?'

'Well, she was a very beautiful woman. At first Isabella incurred the hostility of Henry Tudor but perhaps his conscience pricked him, for she was soon confirmed in all her rights and estates. Four years later, Isabella reluctantly accepted Lord Montague as her second husband.' Lady Alice ran her hand along the marble top of the tomb. 'By then Candleton Hall was almost a place of pilgrimage for the Tudor court. There were even rumours that the King had a softness for the Lady Isabella. The marriage to Montague appears to have been happy enough: he died suddenly, in 1502, of an accident in the forest. Lady Isabella, however, was confirmed in her rights as lord of the manor and the estates around. She was visited by the King and his son, the future Henry VIII. She was an old woman when the Reformation occurred but she eagerly cooperated with the dissolution of the nearby monastery of Greyfriars and was given most of their lands.'

'And she had no children?' Emma asked.

'None whatsoever.'

'And on her death?'

'The manor reverted to her first husband's younger brother, there being no other heirs of her body.'

Oliver listened intently. He stole a glance down the church but he could glimpse nothing there. Churches were sacred places but he had never subscribed to the belief that ghosts, malignant or otherwise, were excluded from hallowed ground. Why should they pay service in death to what they'd totally ignored in life?

'But there was a surviving child of Sir Henry?' he asked.

'Ah yes, Mathilda the seamstress. She lies buried in the crypt. Come, I'll show you that now.'

They left the sanctuary. Lady Alice lit a candelabra on the table and opened the crypt door.

'Go slowly,' she warned. 'The steps are steep.'

Oliver followed her into the cold darkness, the candle shedding a pool of light around Lady Alice. He recalled the coffin on the cart as he'd approached the Hall.

'You've had a death recently?'

'Ah yes, an accident. Poor Bennington. He was a mason working on the stone behind the altar. He came down here and slipped on those steps. You can see they are steep and jagged.'

Lady Alice's voice sounded hollow, sepulchral. Oliver did not like the crypt with its cold, dank and eerie walls and atmosphere. At the bottom of the steps Lady Alice, with Meddlecott's help, lit candles fixed in iron sockets on the wall, yet these only emphasised the long, dancing shadows. The crypt stretched under the church and probably out into the graveyard.

'It's really a mausoleum,' Lady Alice observed.

She pointed to the plaques and tablets on the wall commemorating those Seatons who had fought and died for their country in the navy or in the colonies abroad. Many of the flagstones also served as funeral slabs; tombs ranged throughout the crypt. Some were simply stone plinths, others bore effigies, many were crumbling, their inscriptions faded with age.

Lady Alice led them into the darkness and stopped at a square, stone tomb. It bore no ornamentation, only a faded inscription on the side above pious exclamations from the psalter.

'This is Mathilda Seaton's tomb. The rest . . .' Lady Alice sighed. 'Well, we have a copious library and records. Seatons have been buried here since the reign of Henry I.'

'And where is the Lady Isabella's grave?'

'There isn't one.'

Abruptly the crypt grew darker. The flames of the candle diminished as they danced in the coldness which swept through.

'I beg your pardon?'

Lady Alice closed her eyes. 'On the morning of 1st July 1554 Lady Isabella Seaton heard Mass and went for her usual morning ride. A few hours later the servants, alarmed at their mistress's failure to return, went out looking for her. Her horse was found down near the mere, her veiled headdress in the water, and that was it. Lady Isabella had disappeared. She was never seen again. According to records, the countryside was searched; troops were even sent from Norwich to assist. They say Isabella was thrown from her horse and drowned. Her remains probably lie somewhere out in the mere; the bottom is a tangled mess of weeds, so it would be easy for a corpse to be lost there.'

'These records?' Oliver asked. 'They are accessible? As I will explain later, I need to study them.'

He jumped and Lady Alice gave a scream as the crypt door slammed shut, the force extinguishing some of the candles.

'A draught,' Meddlecott hastened to explain. 'A draught from the main door to the church.'

'We didn't leave it open,' Emma said. She turned. 'Can you hear that?'

At first Oliver thought it was an illusion but then he heard it, a woman singing, the voice rather harsh and guttural.

'It's a Goliard song,' Oliver declared. 'One of those student songs from the Middle Ages, "*Phoebus Clarus*"!'

They stood and listened. The singing grew stronger as if the woman was now outside the door at the top of the steps.

'Is anyone there?' Lady Alice called.

The door opened, swinging back with a crash on its hinges. Meddlecott, followed by Oliver, leapt up the steps only to find the church deserted. The priest, however, was sure he caught a fragrance, a strange perfume, sickly sweet, which hung like incense in the air. Meddlecott was pale, rather shaken. Lady Alice and Emma came up the steps.

'I don't know about you,' the doctor muttered, 'but, Lady Alice, I'm starving and I certainly need a drink.'

They left the church. Lady Alice locked it and they walked the short distance back to the Hall.

The night was freezing. The full moon, slipping in and out of the clouds, sparkled on the hoar frost on the grass. Silence, no bird song, not even an owl hoot. Oliver was sure that they were being watched as the terrors which lurked at Candleton began to manifest themselves.

They supped in the small dining hall where the fire had been built up. Lady Alice's cooks served up a tureen of boiling hot soup, slices of roast beef, dishes of vegetables, baked and roasted potatoes. Father Oliver said grace. Stokes, portly and pompous, instructed the maids to serve while hovering over his mistress like a guardian angel. Oliver knew from Lady Alice's warning glance that they were not to discuss anything. It was not until the meal was over, coffee and liqueurs being served, that all the servants left the dining room except for Stokes: he closed the door and stood guarding it like a sentry.

'You've been here a few hours,' Lady Alice began, not raising her eyes. 'You appreciate that you are not here on a wild goose chase?'

Oliver sipped at his port and nodded. He was more

concerned by what he had seen during the meal – shapes, shadows flitting across the far side of the room.

'I don't believe all this,' Meddlecott broke in. 'Phantasms of the mind, Lady Alice's nerves are frayed.' He watched as Emma opened her small handbag and brought out a leather-bound notebook and pencil. 'Are you going to record, Mistress Grafeld, everything we say?'

'I hope not,' Emma smiled.

'What is your married name?' he asked.

'Purcell,' Emma replied. 'My husband's name was Felix Purcell. I was honoured to use it but I reverted to Grafeld. It makes things simpler for those who wonder or become suspicious.'

Oliver put his glass of port down. 'I wonder,' he began, 'if some hauntings are just recordings of the past?' The priest pointed to a wine stain on the tablecloth. 'That occurred about an hour ago, at the beginning of the meal, but its effect is still with us. It tastes of wine, it smells of wine and, if examined by a chemist, he would declare it is wine. For all I know there might be a process whereby that stain could become wet again.'

'What are you implying?' Meddlecott asked.

'First, there are living, active ghosts,' Oliver replied. 'A soul which is earthbound can still intervene in our affairs as we can in theirs though I cannot describe the process. Secondly, ghosts, like that wine stain, might be phenomena from the past which, in certain circumstances, can be reawakened.'

'Like what we heard in the church?' Lady Alice asked.

'A good example. Now, that door could have been slammed and that song sung to taunt us. Or it could have been an act or incident which took place hundreds of years ago.'

'But why now?' Meddlecott asked. 'These phenomena have only recently begun!'

'They may have occurred before for all we know. However, let's revert to the first kind of haunting, a malignant presence.

Something has happened in this Hall to give this being strength, to make it believe it could intervene in our affairs.' Oliver sipped on his port. 'And that brings us to you, Lady Alice . . .'

She sighed and looked round. 'Stokes,' she called out. 'I'd be grateful if you'd leave us now. Make sure none of the servants eavesdrop.'

Stokes bowed and left quietly as a shadow. Lady Alice waited until the door closed behind him.

'Father, I know you are going to question me about my husband's death and what has happened since. Thomas was a good man, a benevolent landlord, well liked and respected by his tenants and his peers. He was not a man of prayer but . . .'

Oliver noticed she avoided Meddlecott's gaze.

'But he loved the Hall. His greatest disappointment was that we didn't have a living child.'

'And his death?' Oliver asked.

'In September last there was a big meet of the Candleton hunt. My husband was not a well man: he had served for a while on the east coast of Africa and suffered from a tropical disease which would strike without warning, leaving him depleted. But Thomas was Thomas. He insisted on going out with the hunt, and his horse failed to clear a hedge. Thomas should never have tried it. The horse was severely injured and had to be destroyed. Thomas's neck snapped like a twig. He lies buried in the cemetery. I often . . .' Her voice trailed off.

Oliver looked at Emma, who was quietly taking notes.

'And since then?' he asked.

'I will answer for Lady Alice,' Meddlecott spoke up.

'No, no, William!' Lady Alice raised her hand. 'I intend to tell Father Oliver the truth. My husband and I, well, often times we did not lie together, like husband and wife. But, shortly before his death, we did.' Lady Alice bit her lip. 'At first I couldn't believe it but, Father Oliver, I am with child. I must be approaching my third month.' She blinked back the tears. 'One of the great ironies of my life,' she whispered, wiping away the tears, 'is that I feel this baby is safe yet my husband, who so passionately wanted a child, did not live to see it. I am worried, Father, by these phenomena. I don't know if my husband's death, the conception of a child, or my mind or soul are the cause of these happenings, the tapping, the walking, that awful face. I want them to end!'

'It will not be easy,' Oliver said. 'Tomorrow evening, my lady, I might conduct an exorcism, that may or may not be successful. Or . . .'

'Or what?' Meddlecott snapped.

'It might even make matters worse. What I must do,' Oliver insisted, 'is discover the roots of this haunting. It's like a weed in a garden. You may take off the stalk and the leaves but, if the roots are left, the weeds will reappear even stronger.'

'So, where do you propose to begin?'

'The little I know lies in what is called the Spanish Chamber, Lady Isabella's room. I also need to study the records and archives. This Hall hides great secrets and I need to dig them out.'

'But why is it happening now?' Lady Alice demanded.

'I don't know. I really don't. Tomorrow I'll begin. In the meantime, Lady Alice, you must remain calm. Dr Meddlecott, you don't seem convinced?'

'I'm a country physician, Father, I don't belong to your religion and, to misquote Hamlet, I do not believe that there is more to life than what is contained in your philosophies. I also know something about the power of the mind. Lady Alice is very tense. She has suffered a grievous mishap, she is expecting a child at a time when . . .' He shook his head. 'When that seemed impossible. This talk of ghosts. Why should we accept it?'

'That's a very good question, Doctor. Why, as well as why now and, above all, what does this haunting intend?'

'Intend?'

'Yes, hauntings can take place for a variety of reasons. In the Old Testament the ghost of Samuel came back to warn Saul. The ghost of Hamlet's father returned to demand justice and retribution.'

'So, why not begin now?' Meddlecott teasingly asked. 'Discover the cause of all this.'

'I am not ready,' Oliver replied. 'And I will only begin when I think it is right.' He pushed back his chair, stretching his legs which hurt after the journey and the ride earlier in the afternoon. His eyes were also growing weary.

Meddlecott took out a cigar, snipped off the end and busied himself lighting it; small rings of fragrant tobacco filled the room.

Oliver finished his port.

'Is your sister your secretary?' Lady Alice asked, watching Emma still making notes.

'Secretary, housekeeper,' Oliver said. 'My guardian angel.'

'If I wasn't here,' Emma declared, continuing to write, 'Oliver would go out without his socks and shoes!'

Oliver sat back in his chair and laughed. He was about to respond when his eye caught the wine stain he had pointed out earlier. It was liquefying, turning into a thick oozy mess, like blood on a butcher's stall. He stared in fascination: flies appeared from nowhere, black and bloated, to hover above the growing dark-red pool. Lady Alice had also seen them and covered her mouth with her hand. Meddlecott jumped to his feet.

'*In nomine Christi*,' Oliver murmured. 'In the name of Christ, leave us!'

A rush of cold air brushed the nape of his neck as if the freezing night air were pouring through an open window. Oliver glanced at the tablecloth. The pool of blood was widening for the flies to feast on. He made the sign of the cross. As he did so, an insistent tapping rattled the windows and, against the far wall, a scrabbling could be heard, as if someone with long nails was scratching at the plaster. The priest closed his eyes, bowing his head in prayer.

'In Christ's name!' he whispered. 'Go back to the place of darkness whence you've come!'

Oliver opened his eyes. Lady Alice sat horrorstruck. Meddlecott, holding his cigar, was gaping open-mouthed. Emma looked frightened, gripping the notebook in two hands as if it was a shield against what was coming. Oliver again blessed the table and, within the twinkling of an eye, the pool of blood and the flies reverted to an ordinary wine stain on a white tablecloth.

The rapping on the window, however, was more insistent. Oliver walked across to open the casement shutter. The wind caught at his breath; he closed his eyes at the dry leaves which whirled in. He stood his ground, lifting his hand to protect his face, gazing over his fingers into the darkness.

A horse-rider, hooded and cloaked, its mount moving restlessly, was standing out on the path. Then the horse galloped away, the sound of its hooves fading like the knell of a funeral bell.

Oliver slammed the window shut and turned towards the table. Lady Alice, Meddlecott and Emma were all staring at him. He glanced at his chair: the Presence was sitting there, hiding beneath its high back. A hand came out, vein-streaked, gnarled, spotted with age. It reminded Oliver of the hand he had seen in Velasquez's painting *The Dead Knight*; it grasped the arm of the chair, a golden bracelet round the slim wrist just beneath a dark-blue cuff.

Oliver could tell from Emma's face that she could see nothing. He stopped.

'Say your prayers,' he murmured. 'Quietly to yourselves with all the faith you can muster.'

Emma recited the *Ave Maria*. Lady Alice joined in, Meddlecott's lips moved wordlessly. Oliver slowly approached the chair but, when he looked over the back, there was nothing. The hand had disappeared. Had it existed in the first place, he wondered? Or was it a figment of his imagination?

'Priest! Priest! Varlet priest!' The words came hissing like a spiteful child trying to frighten.

The two women stopped their prayers and followed the priest's gaze. On the white tablecloth was a message daubed in wine: 'Do you think, canting priest, that I be a-feared of you?'

Chapter 6

Oliver brushed the wine with his fingers. Meddlecott relit his cigar, trying to control his trembling fingers.

'Father, I apologise.' He blew a smoke ring. 'I have seen more in the last half hour than many do in a lifetime. What is happening? It's so frightening!'

'It is and it isn't,' Oliver replied. 'What you are seeing is trickery, sleight of hand, games from a sideshow.'

'But why?' Lady Alice asked. 'What does it mean?'

Oliver stretched over to the decanter and, trying to ensure his hand didn't tremble, refilled his glass of port.

'A Presence haunts Candleton,' he continued. 'As in a game of chess, this Presence is now making its opening moves. The spirit world is not unlike our own, just the other side of the mirror. The Presence, whatever or whoever it is, wants to frighten us. Anxiety is the best means to beat its opponents down and then attack. In the Gospels Christ was tempted when He was fasting alone in the desert: He was vulnerable, mentally and physically at His weakest. This is what is happening here.'

'But how can they move? The rapping? The writing?'

Oliver shrugged. 'I've seen conjuring tricks, illusions, the power of the mind. Soldiers from India talk of the fakirs, wise men who can disappear up ropes, draw blood from walls. A ghost is still a being with a mind and will of its own.'

'Is it dangerous?' Lady Alice asked.

He was going to shake his head but Lady Alice held his gaze.

'Yes, they are. They can frighten as well as release a form of energy. When I was in Valladolid I attended an exorcism in the cathedral. A young bull fighter, who claimed he was haunted, even possessed, by the ghost of a dead rival.

'The exorcism was carried out by a learned friar. During the rite the exorcist must tell the spirit where to go. A young nobleman was in attendance; he didn't believe anything he saw. When the spirit began to scream, "Where can I go? Where can I go?", this young fop called out, "Well you can come to me!" I wouldn't have believed it if I hadn't seen it with my own eyes. There was a rushing sound like a strong wind. The young man was picked up and hurled at least nine yards across the nave. He was severely bruised, concussed and, for five days, lost the power of speech. We must be careful,' Oliver concluded. 'Say our prayers, have faith and do nothing which will indulge or strengthen the power of the Presence.'

Oliver finished his port and got to his feet.

'Lady Alice, Dr Meddlecott, it has been a strenuous day. I have one favour to ask. I would like to walk around the Hall tonight. May I have a key to the Spanish Chamber?'

Lady Alice nodded. 'I'll send it up to you, Father.'

Oliver bade them all goodnight and walked out. He was half-way up the stairs when he heard his name called. Stokes stood at the foot of the stairs.

'Are we in danger, Father? The servants, they are already talking about Bennington's death.'

'We are always in danger, Stokes,' Oliver replied. 'So be circumspect. Are you a man of prayer?'

'No, Father, but,' for once the butler smiled, 'I think I am about to undergo a conversion.' He walked up to meet the priest. 'Can you really help her ladyship?'

'God willing. Tell me, has this ever happened before?'

Stokes fingered a wing of his high, starched collar.

'I've been here twenty-seven years. I've never seen the likes nor heard the sounds which I have over the last few weeks. However, in the village is a very old woman, Agatha Turnbull.

She must be ninety years old. One of the gardeners who drinks at the Black Swan says that Agatha used to talk about a haunting which took place at the Hall in her younger days.' The butler raised one shoulder. 'That's all I've heard.'

Grafeld thanked him and went up to his own chamber. He lit the candles on either side of the crucifix as well as those on the candelabra near the bed. Opening his breviary he read the Compline until there was a knock on the door and Stokes came in with the key to the Spanish Chamber.

After he'd gone Oliver stared out through the window. The night was cold, the panes were already frosted. Oliver wondered what Emma thought of Dr Meddlecott. The priest worried constantly about his sister and her devotion to him. Was it true what she said? Had he ever grown up? Or had something died that terrible afternoon when he and Arthur had sheltered under an oak as the fire fell from Heaven?

Since then, everything had radically changed. He had been studious but, by the time he was sixteen, he was described as very shy, a bookworm. He smiled. Was it shyness or did he really like people? And this gift of his? Was Emma right? Should he concentrate more on becoming a parish priest? Would his 'gift', as they termed it, ever leave him? What would happen if it did? Would his faith go as well?

Oliver looked at the clock on the mantelpiece. It was not yet midnight. He had drunk a little too much port; his eyes grew heavy. He dozed for a while on the bed and, when he awoke, was lying on his side. He turned over, worried about the candles, and stared into the ghoulish face of an old woman.

Oliver flailed around on the bed. He had never seen a look of such quiet malice: the face was long, the lips prim, firmly pressed together, the eyes were burning coals. Oliver's throat went dry, he couldn't even recall a prayer. He stared at the apparition, aware of how freezing cold the room had grown, while out of the corner of his eye he saw the curtains billow and realised every window had been opened.

'Get thee gone, priest!' The words came in a rustle of foul breath. The heavy-lidded eyes closed and the vision disappeared.

Oliver scrambled off the bed. He closed the windows, removed the fire guard and threw some coal on to the glowing cinders. He clumsily used the bellows to stoke up the flames, then took the coverlet from the bed and wrapped it round his shoulders.

For a while he just knelt, his mind a jumble of images and words. He remembered a favourite phrase from the Jesus Psalter which he kept repeating until the warmth returned to his hands and body.

Oliver put the fire guard back. He checked that everything in the room was secure and, taking his cane and a small crucifix, opened the door and walked along the gallery. There was no light from under Emma's door but Lady Alice had not yet retired. The clock in the hall below chimed one.

Oliver walked into the darkness, clasping the cross, which made him feel secure. He went round the Hall. On two occasions he startled maids and others going about their last duties before they retired. Oliver murmured his apologies. He was relieved to meet Stokes who was carrying out a final tour of the house. The butler kindly agreed to escort him down to the Spanish Chamber and, after the priest had unlocked the door, lit the candelabra inside before bidding Oliver goodnight.

The priest sat at the table near the window and gazed around. He appreciated this truly gothic chamber. The Spanish leather gave off a strange, fragrant perfume. The silence was not oppressive but calm. Oliver gazed across at the portrait on the wall; beside it the glass covering the tapestry sparkled and gleamed in the candlelight.

'What have we here?' the priest murmured.

He sat concentrating, his eyes never leaving the tapestry. As he did so he grew aware of a deep sadness, of someone who had left with business unfinished, sins unforgiven. Other impressions surfaced, clamouring voices at the back of his mind.

He looked out of the window. At first he thought the shadow of a tree lay across the path but, as he stared, he could make out a figure of a man. Surely it was the same apparition he had seen earlier in the day?

'What are you doing here? Why do you meddle?'

The words shattered the silence like the crack of a whip. Oliver, startled, rose to his feet. He picked up the candelabra and stared around. No one was there. He walked towards the tapestry and its strange scenes sprang to life. He moved to the side and, summoning up his courage, studied the portrait. He recognised the same face, the same piercing eyes he had seen when he had first awoken. They seemed to have a life of their own.

'You are my enemy!'

The words echoed in the priest's brain. He had not begun to do his research but he knew this was the Presence. He would have to combat her and she would prove to be a redoubtable opponent.

Oliver left the room without further incident. When he returned to his bedroom, he was surprised to see Emma, a rather over-sized dressing gown about her, sitting in one of the chairs.

'Sister, you should be asleep.'

'Oliver, don't try to be stern, it doesn't suit you and you know you can't sustain it.'

He sat down on the side of the bed, unbuttoned his waistcoat and kicked off his shoes.

'I know, I know, I'm supposed to untie the laces first.'

'How many cases have you investigated, Oliver?'

He ran his fingers through his hair.

'Since my ordination? Well, it must be about thirty. Most of them were nothing, possibly more if you include people playing games or allowing their imaginations to run riot. You should know, Emma, you've been with me.'

'This is the worst, isn't it?'

Oliver nodded.

'I've read a few books by ghost hunters,' he replied. 'They say ghosts are affected by their surroundings. If a place is destroyed or radically changed, it helps sever the link between the ghost and the place it haunts. That's why I recommended Benfleet's house in the Seven Dials be razed to the ground.' Oliver heard an owl hoot and stared through the window. 'But a place like Candleton? Well, it's like the Tower of London. If we went back four hundred years we would recognise most of it; the walls, the floors, the ceilings have not changed. These have soaked in the atmosphere of the years. Do you remember when we went to see the battlefield at Edgefield?'

'A ghostly place,' Emma replied. 'You could almost imagine the clash of steel, the cries of the dying.'

'Edgefield was one of the fiercest battles of the Civil War. A savage clash between Cavalier and Roundhead. Weeks after the battle many people reported how, in the sky, they could see the battle still being played out. Something like that is happening here though I don't know the reason why.'

'Lady Alice?' Emma asked.

'Possibly. She's highly nervous and anxious. On the one hand she grieves for her husband, on the other she looks forward to the birth of a healthy child. There's something else . . .'

The priest paused at the creak of timber outside the door. He tiptoed and opened it, but there was no one there. He closed the door and came back.

'The Presence here is evil and malignant. I suspect it is Lady Isabella Seaton. Was Sir Thomas's death last autumn due to her? I strongly suspect that poor Bennington's was. However, when I visited the chamber below, I suddenly realised that perhaps there are other presences in the house. Ghosts of people involved in this tragedy.'

He held his hand up, fingers splayed out. 'Think of Lady

Isabella Seaton as the hub of a wheel. As she turned and whirled, the others, like spokes in a wheel, had to follow. As it was in life, so it is in death. Anyway,' Oliver said as he took off his jacket, 'how do you find our good doctor?'

He almost knew the response Emma would make, and sure enough her head came up, chin jutting out.

'He's personable enough, a pleasant man. Do you know he spent some time in London? He was betrothed but his fiancée died in one of the cholera epidemics. He told me a strange story about this place.' Emma was eager to hurry on. She loved her brother but resented his attempts to marry her off. For what would he do without her?

She stared at him, sitting there on the edge of the bed, clothes rumpled, that gentle face creased in concern. He shouldn't be here! He should have nothing to do with this evil but be in some country parish, tending a garden and looking after God's faithful.

Oliver raised his head. 'Emma, I'm waiting!'

'Ah yes.' She got up, wrapping the dressing gown tighter about her. 'After you left Meddlecott made a bit of a confession. He asked Lady Alice if she had ever visited the ruins on that small island in the centre of the lake. She said no, Sir Thomas had always discouraged it.'

'And?'

'Meddlecott declared how Sir Thomas had informed him the small ruins on the island were haunted: that, if you visited them, the mere might not let you back. Dr Meddlecott decided to see for himself . . .'

'And?'

Emma shrugged. 'He found the ruins lonely, eerie but, while poling the skiff back, he inexplicably fell off. Only the intervention of Sir Thomas saved him from drowning.' She paused. 'So, for God's sake, as well as mine, Oliver, please be very, very careful!'

After an uneventful night Oliver woke late. Emma was already waiting in the small dining room. Stokes informed them that Lady Alice had decided to stay in her room that morning.

A sumptuous breakfast was laid out on silver platters along the sideboard: eggs, bacon, sausage, potatoes, dried kippers, muffins and thick slices of bread. They ate in silence, Stokes hovering around to ensure all was well.

Oliver and Emma then went for a short walk in front of the house before crossing the bridge. They visited the chapel, not as daunting as the previous evening with the December sunlight streaming through the stained glass windows. On their return to the house Stokes took them into the muniment room, a small panelled chamber adjoining the library.

'Lady Alice believes you will have no problems.' The butler afforded a slight smile. 'Her ladyship knows that you are a history scholar.' He pointed to the iron-bound coffers scattered round the chamber as well as the rolls of parchment in small pigeon-holes in the great racks around the walls. 'The unpublished manuscripts are all here. Just inside the library, you'll find the printed histories of Candleton.' Stokes gestured at the travelling clock on the mantelpiece. 'At eleven o'clock I'll bring you refreshments and a maid will call in to ensure the fire burns well.'

'It's warm enough,' Emma declared. She stared up at the small oaken candelabra which hung from the high ceiling. 'This is a beautiful room, one made for a scholar.' She stared fondly as her brother eagerly took out a large calfskin tome from one of the coffers.

'Sir Thomas's father was a skilled antiquarian and historian,' Stokes said. 'You'll find everything arranged and easy to find. Lady Alice mentioned that you would be interested in the Tudor period.' He pointed to a chest beneath the rack of pigeon-holes. 'Her ladyship said you should find most of the records in there.' He bowed and closed the door behind him.

'I'm not very good at Latin or Tudor English,' Emma grinned. 'No, that's a lie, brother, I couldn't read them at all.'

'You study the published histories,' Oliver suggested. 'I'll search the manuscripts.'

Oliver was soon lost in his favourite world: household books, letters and other documents from the Seaton archives. At first he couldn't resist simply surveying what the small record office held. After listening to Emma read out extracts from the published history, he concentrated on the household rolls, letters, bills and memoranda from when Lady Isabella Seaton had ruled Candleton as ruthlessly as any medieval baron.

A great deal of the information was simply lists of goods bought, rents due from outlying farms, gifts at Christmas and Easter. Others were more telling. Oliver soon discovered that Sir Henry had been smitten by his new wife, Isabella. Payments were made for jewels; cloth of gold for her dresses; a hamper of spices from the port of Bishop's Lynn; palfreys from the great horse market at Smithfield. Her chambers were refurbished and redecorated and, when Isabella travelled to Our Lady's shrine at Walsingham, a great retinue of servants followed.

Henry and Isabella's marriage had taken place just before the Yorkist cause collapsed and the Tudors swept to the throne. King Edward IV had visited Candleton, as had the great barons of the Council: Sir Henry feasted and dined them all.

In one household book, Oliver came across a dramatic entry from the spring of 1483. 'To Robert Halstead 5 shillings for bringing the news of the death of good King Edward to Candleton.'

After Edward IV's death the Seatons grew more secretive. The new King Richard III and his lieutenant John Howard, Duke of Norfolk, were in constant communication with

Candleton but so were other visitors – 'from across the seas', according to the household record. Oliver put his pen down.

'A dangerous time,' he said.

'What's that, brother?'

'Edward IV died. His brother Richard usurped the throne. The Seatons had no choice but to support him. However, I suspect they also entertained Tudor agents, playing both ends against the middle.'

Oliver returned to his studies. Another name now appeared in the records: Lord Montague, Henry's very distant cousin. He often supped and stayed at the Hall for days: an honoured guest, Lord Montague was lavishly rewarded with presents.

Oliver continued to make his notes. A maid came in and put some more pine logs on the fire. Stokes brought cups of hot chocolate and, just before noon, Lady Alice herself made a brief visit. She stood, one hand resting on Father Oliver's shoulder.

'I slept well last night,' she laughed. 'The first time for weeks. No phenomena, no haunting!' Lady Alice patted the priest. 'That's your doing, Father.'

Oliver winked at Emma. He did not wish to contradict Lady Alice. Nevertheless, he recalled what he had seen the previous evening and knew the haunting would return with added vehemence.

They worked on with a brief respite for lunch. Oliver could hardly remember what he ate, so immersed was he in his task. Stokes came back late in the afternoon to remind him that Lady Alice would like Mass celebrated in the chapel about six o'clock. Oliver, distracted, agreed and went back to his studies, building up pictures of the Hall under Lady Isabella's steward-ship between 1485 and her sudden disappearance in 1554. He was looking for more letters when he noticed the brown leather wallet, ingrained with dust, at the bottom of the chest. He picked this out. Inside was a slim calfskin tome with ten pieces of parchment sewn together and held between two leather covers. On the first page was written *Petrus Rivers me scripsit.*

'Peter Rivers.' Oliver lifted his head and stared at Emma, who had her head buried in one of the volumes from the library.

'Peter Rivers, I recognise that name. Ah yes, he was one of the chaplains. If I remember rightly, he was here some time?'

Oliver turned over the pages. Most of the documents he had read had been written in Latin or Norman French, the abbreviations clearly understandable and easy to translate. This was different. The letters were all jumbled. Oliver skimmed through the book and, putting it down, went to the small box of index cards which listed the contents of each case. At last he found the title he was looking for.

'A journal written by Peter Rivers, chaplain to the Seaton family and vicar of the chapel, 1483–1555. This was the only benefice he held; apparently a man of great sanctity who died in his 93rd year. The journal is written in cipher, I can trace different dates but nothing more.'

Oliver put the card back and stood, fingers to his lips. He'd come across Peter Rivers' name on countless occasions in the manuscripts. Rivers celebrated Masses, looked after the spiritual welfare of the household and the peasants who worked the farms. A valued and high-ranking retainer of the Seatons, the chaplain had been well respected, keeping himself free of the many vices so common to the clergy of the time.

Oliver gripped the calfskin tome between his hands and stared down at it. He felt a thrill of excitement. This was the chaplain's private journal, probably written as a means of expressing the secrets of the Seaton household without breaking confidence. Oliver opened the book. Could he break the cipher used? He had come across ciphers in different manuscripts in Spain as well as England and sometimes they were impossible to crack.

Oliver stared out of the window. The weak sunlight was fading and a mist was slipping over the parkland. He glimpsed the figure staring in at him, a young man dressed in fifteenth-century attire: jerkin, hose and mud-stained boots, a cloak around his shoulders, the cowl pulled over his head. It was the same person Oliver had glimpsed before, young, thin-faced, wild-eyed, gripping a dagger.

'Who is that?' Oliver whispered.

'Oliver, stop talking to yourself!' Emma snapped. She closed the book she had been reading, keeping her finger in the pages. 'I've just read something . . .'

'What?' Oliver glanced out of the window, but the young man had vanished.

Emma opened the book, smoothing down the pages.

'Apparently the Seatons supported the Royalist cause in the Civil War. After the Restoration in 1660, Sir James Seaton came back into his own. He'd spent the years of Cromwell's rule with his master King Charles II in France. There, Sir James fell in love and married a beautiful French noblewoman, Thérèse, whom he brought back to Candleton.'

'And?'

'For fifteen years they had a happy, almost idyllic, life until Sir James was killed in a mysterious accident here at Candleton. According to reports Thérèse's mind became unhinged. She experienced hallucinations and phantasms. Eerie hauntings took place at night; voices were heard shrieking; dark figures seen around the house. Now her son chose to ignore it but Thérèse brought in a vicar, Walter Hobard. An exorcism took place. There are not many details but it was unsuccessful. On the following day Hobard was found drowned in the lake.'

Oliver tried to control his shivers.

'Continue.'

'Thérèse's behaviour became the talk of the county. Her son did not wish her to be sent to Bedlam so a small cottage was built on the island in the centre of the lake. Thérèse was placed there. The haunting stopped but Lady Thérèse's situation grew worse. She claimed the ghosts had followed her.' Emma's voice dropped to a whisper. 'One morning she was found hanged from a beam in the cottage.'

Oliver sat back in his chair.

'Apparently,' Emma continued, 'her death caused consternation. She was a Catholic yet she had committed suicide and could not be interred in consecrated ground, so they buried her out on the island. Her grave is still there.' Emma paused. 'And what have you found?'

Oliver rose and paced up and down as he always did when excited.

'It's a detective story.' He picked up the journal. 'Though there's a large piece missing from the picture. This is a journal written in a secret cipher. I intend to translate it though I have a general idea of what happened here.' He paused. 'Imagine, Emma.'

His sister tried to hide her smile as her brother warmed to his subject.

'Imagine,' he repeated. 'The year is 1485, the Seatons are in a real dilemma. Richard III and the House of York demand their allegiance but, like many gentry of the county, they are also in secret negotiation with Henry Tudor in France. Now Sir Henry's cousin, Alain Montague, is a Tudor partisan. King Richard III issued a proclamation, a most notorious one, that all who didn't come to his assistance, when he summoned his army to meet at Nottingham, would be regarded as traitors.

'I can almost pinpoint when the Seatons devised their plot. In April 1485 Lord Montague was here for most of the month, until he abruptly departed as if there had been an argument. In July Sir Henry and Benedict go to join Richard at Nottingham. The other son, Ralph, flees south-west and, with his kinsman Montague, joins the invading army of Henry Tudor.' Oliver waved his hand. 'You know the rest of the story. Sir Henry was executed, Benedict disappeared, while Ralph was killed at Bosworth.' Oliver paused. 'For a while Lady Isabella was in mourning. Somehow she managed to keep her estates and the price she paid was marriage to her kinsman Montague who took the Seaton name.' He tapped the table-top. 'Strange, isn't it? The present Lady Seaton's husband was killed in a riding accident? Well, so was Lord Montague, while Sir James in the seventeenth century met a similar fate.'

'Is that possible?' Emma asked.

'It could be a family curse. Three of William the Conqueror's sons died in hunting accidents. Anyway, Lady Isabella grew into a formidable woman. Kings and bishops paid her reverence . . .'

'Did she love anyone?' Emma asked.

'No. She grieved for her first husband and for her second but what comes through, very clearly, is her great passion for Candleton Hall.'

'And her disappearance?'

'I found references to it. The Duke of Northumberland was in power then, Protector of young Edward VI. A time of great turbulence in Norfolk because the county was still Catholic and supported Mary Tudor. Search parties were sent out but she was never found. The manor was inherited by another in the Seaton line. Well, that's how the story unfolds.'

'But?'

Oliver pulled a face. 'But I think it's all wrong: deep in my heart, I believe Lady Isabella was personally responsible for all the deaths in her family.'

Chapter 7

After Mass in the chapel, Father Oliver, Emma and Lady Alice had dinner in the small dining room. Dr Meddlecott joined them just after the first course had been served. Oliver had fasted before Mass; now he only ate a little soup and some cold meats.

Once darkness had fallen they ended the meal hurriedly, Stokes clearing the servants away from the main part of the Hall. Under Oliver's directions, the butler set up a small altar at the far end of the first gallery. A bitterly cold breeze seeped through the cracks and made the candle flames leap in some eerie dance.

Oliver put on a surplice and stole and, taking his copy of the *Rituale Romanum*, stood before the altar. He crossed himself and, his gaze fixed on the crucifix in the centre of the white cloth, intoned the litany of invocation which marked the beginning of an exorcism. He stumbled over the words, feeling unsure. No phenomena had appeared, none of the tell-tale signs that the Powers of Darkness would oppose him, just a sombre, cold gallery illuminated by the candles, its brooding silence broken only by the creak of floorboards.

Emma, Dr Meddlecott and Lady Alice sat in one of the chambers. Both women, at Oliver's request, quietly prayed the rosary, slipping the beads through their fingers.

Oliver finished the litany and tried to compose himself. He picked up the phial of holy water and walked down the gallery sprinkling drops to his left and right. He heard a sound, as if someone were coming up the stairs breathing deeply, slowly, followed by the snarl of an animal, like a dog, cornered, preparing to fight. Oliver, recalling the rite from memory, continued his walk.

'How dare you? How dare a prattling, meddlesome priest come to interfere with me?' The words were a sharp shout.

Oliver didn't know whether they echoed in his own mind or from someone waiting in the darkness. He closed his eyes.

Abruptly all thought of the rite left his mind. Instead he was in a dream. He was in the gallery but it was changed: it was the middle of a day; dust motes danced in the sunshine streaming through the windows. The gallery walls were of white plaster, the floor of black wood covered in crisp green rushes. The chamber doors of the rooms were different. Sounds rose from the yard below; the clip-clop of horses, the cries of ostlers and grooms.

Further along the passageway, a door opened. A tall, majestic woman swept down the gallery. She seemed to glide rather than walk, and was wearing a dark-burgundy dress with a pure white collar. Oliver recognised Lady Isabella. Her face was long and sharp, her veil like that of a nun's coif. She was glaring at him. In her hands she carried an ash cane; keys jangled from the gold, embroidered belt round her slim waist. A woman of power, Oliver thought.

'How dare you?' The woman's lips moved slowly, the words spat out.

Oliver stopped, abashed, not knowing what to do.

The dream changed. He was in the gallery again but it was darker. Lady Isabella was joined by a younger woman, well-dressed but weak-faced and cringing. She was being scolded by Lady Isabella, who beat her roughly across the shoulders with the cane, the crack echoing like the snap of a whip. The young woman backed away sobbing and crying, hands held out to protect herself, but the cane fell again and again.

'Stop it! Stop it!' Oliver shouted.

'Father, what's wrong?'

Lady Alice was standing in the doorway of her chamber. The

priest looked over his shoulder; the candles still glowed but the flame had turned a blueish tinge.

'I'm sorry,' he murmured. 'I don't know. You'd best go back.'

He waited until the door closed and began the invocation again. From below the main door of the Hall opened and shut, the crash echoing through the house. Oliver heard Stokes hurrying from the parlour below.

'Leave it!' the priest shouted, then he was pushed by unseen hands, a vicious prod to his back which sent him staggering forward. He crashed into the wall and turned. A dark shape was hurtling towards him like a plume of black smoke. His face was slapped and the priest smelt the most offensive stench like that from an open sewer or the putrid wastes of that terrible house in Seven Dials.

'Master Benfleet extends greetings!' the voice hissed viciously. 'He sends his regards. He asks will you come back, because he has!'

Oliver tried to control his breathing. Above him he heard a creaking as if someone in the upper gallery was rocking backwards and forwards in a noisy chair. He tried to continue his prayer but his throat had gone dry. He felt a terrible heaviness in his limbs; he tasted blood, its salty tang on his lips. He wiped his mouth.

The hum of flies broke the silence as, bloated, furry, they swarmed round the cut on his mouth. Oliver tried to recall the words of the rite but he couldn't, only a verse of Luke's Gospel: ' "Behold, I have given you power to tread underfoot serpents and scorpions." '

As if in answer something cold and slimy slithered across his ankle. Oliver felt the flies probing his mouth. He lashed out with his boot and made to brush the flies away. Nothing was there.

'He will conceal you,' he murmured, 'with his wings. You will not fear the terrors of the night, nor the arrow that flies by day, nor the plague which prowls in the darkness.' He broke off. That terrible stench was growing, making him catch his breath, he felt as if he was going to be sick. 'Or the scourge that lays waste at noon,' he gasped.

A mocking laugh echoed down the gallery.

'You little, little priest! You clever thing!' The words came in a malevolent whisper. 'Fancy yourself as an exorcist?'

Oliver stared to his left and right. He was no longer sure what he could hear.

'You are not a priest! You are not an exorcist!' The spiteful voice continued. 'You are just a little boy, hiding behind your sister's skirts, frightened of real life. How about a lusty wench to bounce on a bed? Or a flagon of wine to thicken your thin blood?' The voice turned ugly. 'Piss off, priest!'

Oliver was shoved back down the gallery towards the make-shift altar.

'Where are the candles? Where are the candles?' the voice mocked.

Oliver realised he had dropped the holy water. To ease his panic, he crouched down, feeling around on the floor, but there was no longer carpet, only rushes, and they were dried and sharp. He felt pieces of hardened dog turd. Oliver panicked. He drew himself up. For some strange reason he could only think of the chapel, the blessed sacrament in the tabernacle.

He lurched down the gallery, and feathers brushed his face as if some bird of the night had touched him with the tip of its wing. Oliver stopped. He stared up but the ceiling had been ripped off and the cold night sky gazed down at him.

'Where am I?' he muttered. 'Asleep or awake?'

He felt behind him for the wall. His sense of giddiness increased. Someone was coming up the stairs carrying a lantern. Stokes called his name. Oliver staggered on but a face blocked his path. Lady Isabella's, white and vicious, her black eyes glaring.

'Learn your lesson, priest! Do not meddle in things you cannot control!' Her face drew closer. 'Are you frightened? Like a word with Arthur sheltering under that great oak tree when the lightning struck?'

'Go away,' Oliver croaked. 'In Christ's name, leave me alone!'

He drew his fist back but his hand flailed the air. He grasped the carved newel at the top of the banister. Oliver put his foot forward. He felt as if he was back in that house in the Seven Dials looking up instead of looking down. He could hear the awful creaking of that rocking chair and smelt the putrid stench of those graves.

Oliver could take no more. He was about to run but his foot slipped and he crashed down the stairs. He thought of Emma; Archbishop Manning staring at him; Bennington's corpse jolting in its makeshift coffin. His head struck a post and he slipped into unconsciousness.

Even though he was unconscious, Oliver remained aware. He was lying beneath one of the yew trees in the chapel's cemetery. It was a bright spring day. A man was scything the grass around the graves but these were different to what he had seen. Most of the crosses were of wood while the yellow stone of the chapel seemed brighter and cleaner. The roof was of red slate rather than black tiles. The air was sweet with the fragrance of wild flowers. He tried to crawl but found he couldn't. A small, thin friar with balding pate was staring down at him. The man had a severe face but the eyes were kindly. The friar drew his hands from the sleeves of his gown, revealing Ave beads wrapped round his bony fingers.

'Are you ill, Father? Did the fall hurt you?'

The friar crouched down. His eyes were icy blue, slightly watery, as if he had been staring into the wind.

'This is a place of great wickedness,' the friar said quietly. 'I

97

wish I could help you and show you over the wall but I cannot. You must do that for yourself.'

'Why is it wicked?' Oliver asked.

'The sanctuary of sin,' the priest replied, his tone harsher. 'Covetousness and lust, anger, adultery and the most horrid murders!'

'And what can I do?'

'You can rest. You can rest and take your strength.'

A shadow blocked out the sun. It raced across the churchyard as if a huge bird, wings extended, were swooping across to cut off the light. Oliver grew frighteneed. The churchyard was growing dark. The figure with the scythe returned, the face in the cowl was hideous.

'Please help me!' Oliver whispered to the friar.

'I cannot,' the friar replied.

Oliver struggled to his feet but a hand pressed him down.

'Sleep, you must sleep!'

The graveyard grew cold and dark as if drenched in sudden night. Oliver looked up at the sky fearful that the fire might fall again.

'You must sleep!' the voice repeeated.

Oliver closed his eyes. It was so easy to give way, not to struggle, let the darkness take him.

'You must sleep!' Dr Meddlecott declared, staring down at his patient. He pressed his hand against Oliver's face. 'A slight temperature. He's feverish but the sleeping draught I managed to get down him will soon take its effect.'

'He will be well?' Emma pressed Oliver's hand against her face. It was cold and clammy.

Dr Meddlecott sat on the side of the bed and patted her reassuringly on the shoulder. He just wished he could be a little closer, touch the soft smoothness of her neck or gently tug at one of those ringlets.

'What happened last night?' he asked. 'That terrible cold, the stench! It reminded me of a hospital, gangrene and rottenness. I also heard voices.' He touched Emma again on the shoulder. 'You were frightened?'

Emma stared up, her face translucently pale, Meddlecott's heart skipped a beat. She was so beautiful!

'Don't you believe in anything, William?' she asked.

Meddlecott's heart again skipped. He felt a glow of joy: she had called him by his first name!

'I don't know.' He twiddled with his watch which he kept putting in and out of the pocket of his waistcoat. He would say anything to keep her staring at him like that. 'My mother,' he blew his lips out, 'well, she was pious, I suppose, in the conventional sense. My father said there was nothing wrong with a church which couldn't be cured by burning it to the ground and using the land to build a decent hospital.'

Meddlecott made himself more comfortable.

'Once, when I was younger, I became interested. I met a priest working in the slums of Whitechapel, a good man. I also met Mary, who was beautiful. We were betrothed.' He snapped his fingers and glanced away. 'The cholera took her as quickly as a dry leaf in a storm. The little belief I had, well it disappeared like smoke. At first I thought my cynicism was self-indulgent until I was called to the Corpse House, a large, disused shed on the Mile End Road. The hospitals and cemeteries were overflowing and they had to find a place for the mounting pile of cholera corpses.' He paused and tapped his forehead with his hand. 'I'm sorry, I shouldn't be talking of this here.'

'No, continue.'

'Anyway, I went in. The corpses were stacked, blue, decaying, full of rottenness, like a pile of disused weeds. I thought, what is so special about this? What's so sacred about life?' He pulled a face. 'If I had any faith, I left it in that cholera shed!'

'I could turn that on its head,' Emma countered. 'In the midst of such terror, there's always something beautiful, unique.' She leant over, brushing her hand against Oliver's face.

'He'll be well,' Dr Meddlecott reassured her. 'Concussed, he'll have a sore head and weak legs but he'll survive. He has to,' he joked. 'I have got so many questions for him. This gift of his . . .'

'Gift or curse,' Emma replied. 'I'm not too sure what it is.' She pointed her finger playfully at him. 'You propose to tease me? Say why should God give a man such gifts?' Emma's smile faded. 'My husband was a soldier, a very good one. The time we had together was short but very happy. Felix was baptised a Catholic but, like so many soldiers, he had a simple faith, believing duty was the most important virtue. He had an explanation of my brother's gift. He claimed it wasn't so unique. He described how soldiers who had seen a great deal of action develop an intuition about danger, risks, and the unseen.'

'So, your brother has a gift we all have but more developed, like having better eyesight or a stronger heart?'

'Possibly,' Emma replied. 'Though I suppose, if I wasn't his sister and I didn't know what had happened . . .' Her voice trailed off.

Meddlecott waited, fascinated, wanting Emma to make some revelation about her past.

'We were a close family,' she continued slowly, stroking her brother's hand. 'My father was a good, decent man. Mother was French. She had a great joy for life, happiness for her was the garden. She loved flowers. A happy home. There were three children: Arthur the eldest, myself and Oliver.

'Arthur was one of those, well he was a gift from God: always happy, ever ready to help, a good sense of humour. Oh, he could be childish and become fretful but Oliver adored him. There were seven years between them yet where Arthur went Oliver always followed. If Arthur ate an apple, Oliver ate an apple. If

Arthur went fishing, Oliver went fishing.' Her eyes filled with tears. 'At table Mother always said there was an echo in the house. Whatever Arthur said, Oliver would always repeat.

'We were Catholics. Parliament had only recently allowed the Church the right to exist. Arthur devoured all the stories about recusant times. How our priests,' she looked round, 'used to hide in places like this: to say Mass, hear confessions, serve the faithful. It was always the same game. Arthur and Oliver were priests in hiding, I was the sheriff's man.' She brushed her eyes with the back of her hand. 'Arthur used to discover marvellous hiding-places but it wasn't too difficult to find him, because Oliver would always be chattering excitedly. Arthur never complained.

'As he grew older, he pestered Father about sending him abroad to train in Rome, Valladolid or Douai as a priest. Oliver naturally declared he was going too. Then it all changed.' She smoothed the counterpane with her fingers. 'It started so well. A beautiful summer's day in Sussex. We were out in the fields, playing our game of hide and seek. One of those lowering thunderstorms swept in from the Channel. The clouds were low, black as night. Usually we would have run home.'

She glanced up, a faraway look in her eyes.

'It was so strange! On that particular afternoon Oliver became very frightened. Pale, trembling, he stood stock-still. We were beneath an oak tree. He just wouldn't move so we decided to stay with him. The lightning came while the thunder rolled like the roar of a cannon as the rain pelted down.' Emma let go of her brother's hand. 'It happened so quickly. A jagged fork of lightning struck the oak tree. All I could see was a blue flash. Arthur knocking Oliver to the ground. At first I thought he was playing. Oliver picked himself up. He turned Arthur over. Burn marks scorched his left side. I screamed and grabbed Oliver's hand. We ran through the rain-soaked fields.' Emma got to her feet, her face pallid.

'You don't have to tell me this!'

Emma shook her head as she walked towards the window.

'For some strange reason Candleton has revived those memories. Maybe it's the oak trees out in the park or the fact that Arthur and Oliver used to talk about great Catholic houses like this.' She shrugged.

She leant against the windowpane and stared out at the countryside in the grip of a freezing hard frost.

'Arthur must have died instantly. His death broke my parents' hearts. They were never the same again. Within fifteen years both were gone.' She sighed. 'The funeral took place, a priest came from Horsham to say the Requiem Mass. We were all grief-stricken but Oliver, it was terrible! He wouldn't speak, white as a sheet. He used to sit in the parlour looking out of the window as if waiting for Arthur. He'd dress and stand at the foot of the stairs, not just for minutes but for hour after hour. My parents tried to comfort him but Oliver just stared at them. Doctors were called in; they said it was shock and time would heal. My parents thought Oliver's mind was unhinged. They believed they'd lost two sons, not one. Weeks passed into months.'

Emma paused. 'Then it changed again. One night I woke about two o'clock in the morning. It was the feast of All Saints, 1st November. I had taken to sleeping in Oliver's room, and his little cot bed was empty. I tiptoed to the door and listened. Oliver was downstairs. He was not just talking, he was laughing, a deep, merry chuckle like he used to when he and Arthur would plot their games.' She turned. 'I tell you this, William, nothing, and I mean nothing, this Hall can throw at me, can conjure up anything as terrifying as listening to that laugh. I thought my brother had gone mad. I stole downstairs and pushed open the parlour door. Oliver was sitting in Father's chair. He used to do that sometimes, pretending to be Daddy. He was just talking, chattering away. Now and again he'd pause and laugh.'

Meddlecott felt a chill along his back. The beautiful young woman at the window was with him physically but her mind was back in Sussex, sitting in that parlour so many years ago.

' "Oliver, Oliver," I said. "For the love of God what is the matter? Who are you talking to?" He turned, his face as bright as a button. "It's Arthur." He pointed across to an empty chair. "Can't you see? Arthur's come back!" I didn't know what to do. Oliver was so happy, his eyes merry and bright. It was marvellous to see him like that. "And what does Arthur say?" I asked. "He says he's been waiting, waiting so long to see me, at least half an hour." '

Emma joined her hands together. ' "Oliver," I said. "Arthur's dead and has been so for months." "Did you hear that?" Oliver laughed. "No, Arthur says he's only been dead a very short while and he's come to say goodbye to me." The conversation went on like this for about an hour then Oliver got to his feet.' Emma paused. ' "You are going now," he said. He stood smiling, waving his little hand. I thought he would cry or become hysterical but he didn't. He blew the candle out, slipped his hand into mine and trotted back to bed.

'The next morning my parents were delighted. Oliver tried to tell them what had happened. Father became angry so he never raised the matter again.'

'Did Oliver ever tell you what had happened?'

'Oh yes, he couldn't wait to get out of the house, drag me to the bottom of the garden to what we called our "secret place". He said Arthur had woken him up and told him to come downstairs. They had chattered about their games. Arthur said he wasn't frightened, that he was surrounded by friends and that he and they were going on a journey but, before he did, he wanted to say goodbye to him. One day Oliver would follow. Until then Oliver was to study hard and be a good son. If God wanted it, he should become a priest.'

Emma sighed. 'Oliver had always had a very vivid

imagination. I thought he'd dreamt it all so I let him talk. Over the next few months I slowly changed my mind. Oliver's good spirits were restored but he became studious and, for a young boy, very attentive to his spiritual life. By the time he was nine he had already made up his mind to be a priest and wouldn't be shaken from it. He became everything parents want their sons to be and, although they hid it well, they were grief-stricken when he left to study abroad.'

'Did Oliver's gifts become apparent?'

'Oh yes,' Emma murmured absentmindedly. 'It was like water seeping through a gap, drops at first followed by a trickle. He seemed to be able to sense the spiritual moods of other people. One summer Father took us down to the Romney Marshes. We visited a house which was allegedly haunted. Oliver became very frightened. He must have been about thirteen or fourteen then. He adamantly refused to enter the house.

'In the seminary his gifts became more apparent. When he was ordained as a deacon he played a major role in exorcisms. After his ordination to the priesthood, our parents had died, so Oliver came back to England. He wanted to be a parish priest but there was a haunting in Ingatestone in Essex. The official exorcist was ill. Oliver carried it out so successfully that the local bishop wrote to Cardinal Wiseman and, despite his relatively tender years . . .' She shrugged. 'You know the rest: he became an official exorcist to the Catholic hierarchy of England and Wales.'

'Is it always as successful?'

'He's never successful,' Emma retorted. 'He becomes quite angry if you say that. Christ is successful and, if Oliver fails, it's not because the Good Lord fails but because he wasn't prepared or didn't do it right.'

'Like last night?'

'Yes,' Emma sighed, walking back to the bedside. 'That's

happened before but not as violently. When he regains consciousness, Oliver will search his soul for the reason.'

'But you know it already?'

'Yes, I can suspect what happened. Whatever you believe, William, Oliver says evil is like a plant: it has leaves, stem, fruit but, above all, roots. If we have to change ourselves we must pull the evil out, root and branch. We must really convert and the same is true of an exorcism. It's not just a spiritual act. An exorcism also demands those good sound human virtues: clever wit, skill, investigation, stubbornness and a determination to redress wrongs done.'

'So why didn't Oliver wait?'

'He probably wanted to discover the true nature of his adversary. I doubt if he'll try that again until he's more fully prepared. And, before you ask, there is evil buried here at Candleton. Something terrible has happened and it has to be pulled up.' She sat down in a chair and grinned at him. 'Heavens above, I'm sounding more like Mother every day.' She grasped Oliver's hand. 'Ah, good, not so cold. Well,' she added impishly, 'what do you think, William?'

'I have learned colleagues in London,' he replied, 'who would say that Oliver's state of mind, his change in behaviour, his conversation with Arthur, his desire to be a priest, are all the results of shock. That Oliver feels guilty about his brother's death, that he wishes to compensate and make reparation.' He touched the back of Emma's hand. 'And you Catholics, with your sense of sin and guilt, are fertile ground for such ideas.'

'I don't believe that!'

Meddlecott's heart sank at the cold, stubborn look on Emma's face.

'Never once has Oliver felt guilty; frightened, fearful of failure yes, but never guilty!'

'You seem so certain.'

'Do I now, Doctor? Tell me, good physician, what would

your learned colleagues say about my state of mind?'

'A level-headed, intelligent young woman.' Meddlecott would have liked to add more but he was wary of Emma's change of mood.

'Not the sort of woman to see visions?'

'No.'

'Then I'll tell you that I believe Oliver for two reasons. First, my brother has many faults: he can be absentminded and infuriatingly dreamy but he's not a liar.' The stubborn tilt of her chin warned Meddlecott against further observations. 'And the second reason, my good Doctor, and I have told very few people this, I too had a vision.'

'I beg your pardon?'

'Oh yes, the day Oliver left for the seminary. I was very sad so I went for a long walk. I truly missed Oliver. Where he went, I followed, just to look after him. I was always frightened that something might happen to him. I knew about his gifts. He didn't brag about them, in fact the opposite, he said God would use them sometime in the future.

'Anyway, on that particular day, I found myself in the fields walking towards the tree where Arthur had been killed. It was beautiful, warm and very, very quiet. I felt such an ache inside of me. How would Oliver cope in the harsh seminary life? Tired, I sat down on the grass. We'd spent the previous night getting ready for Oliver's departure. I must have gone through his coffers and chests a number of times to ensure he had everything he needed.

'Then I fell asleep, though not for very long. When I awoke, I saw a cluster of butterflies lift and move past the oak tree. I watched them and, out of the corner of my eye, glimpsed a blur of colour.' Emma got to her feet, fighting to control the trembling of her lower lip. 'You know, even before I turned, I realised it was Arthur. He was standing there, hands in his pockets, that lazy smile on his lovely face. "Don't be sad,

Emma," he said. "I've come back. Oliver will come back."
"Why?" I asked. "Look after him, Emmy. Always look after
him." '

She smoothed down the folds of her dress. 'And that's all
I'm going to say.'

Chapter 8

The Presence, which lived in its own world and viewed that of the living as through a glass darkly, rejoiced in the triumph of its own evil will. The Presence swept through the Hall like a prince through his court.

There was now no need to display its power in frightening phenomena or eerie manifestations. A sunset of fiery red colours illuminated images in its existence, bizarre fusions of animals and humans. Birdlike monsters who'd carried knives between their cruel beaks, their torsos made of fish-tails, their humanoid legs shod with cruel spurs. Disembodied hands and stubby limbs; fleeing shadows, dark elementals. The Presence ignored these, concentrating on its own will, on the evil it planned, still holding in thrall, by chains forged over hundreds of years, those who had shared or been beaten down by its wickedness.

In the twinkling of an eye the Presence moved through wall and door to its secret chamber. The place it had always inhabited, where the circle had been drawn, the sacrifices made and the compact with Death and the Dark Lords solemnly sealed.

The Presence revelled in its malice. It now saw no danger from the priest. Its soul had no place for compassion: the forces which had driven it during life still dominated it in death. True, the Presence recognised the priest as a terrible adversary. Yet, over the centuries, others had tried only to fail, because of themselves or because they lacked the will, the commitment to seek out and confront it.

The Presence was determined to show who was the master.

It moved out again, across the park, towards the gaunt, black, outstretched arms of a sycamore tree.

Lucy Gibson, chambermaid at Candleton, sat in the wooden bower, built under the outspread branches of a great sycamore tree, and stared out across the darkening park.

Lucy had just passed her seventeenth birthday. She regarded herself as very fortunate that she had secured such good employment at Candleton. Lady Alice was a kindly mistress, generous and not too severe. Lucy now had high hopes. She'd caught the eye of Tom Weston, a young footman who dressed smartly and prided himself on either succeeding Stokes at Candleton or, perhaps, being butler at one of the other great houses in the country. They had met and kissed in shadowy corners on dark staircases. Tom had pressed himself fiercely against her, his hands going, well, it was best not to think of that.

Lucy pulled her cape and hood closer and swung her legs backwards and forwards. She definitely looked her best in a grey linen dress and crisp white petticoats. Yes, the mirror couldn't lie: with her blonde ringlets, small sweet face, slim hips and swelling breasts, Lucy always drew the glances of other men but it was Tom Weston who ruled her heart. If only he'd be more serious! Tom was for ever playing practical jokes. Lucy tightened her generous mouth into a thin, bloodless line. Well, Tom had better not play such tricks on her.

He'd told her to meet him here in this arbour. It had been built by some lord of Candleton years ago, so, if anyone was caught out in the rain while walking in the park, they could take shelter. It was now a famous trysting place. Cook had told her to be careful of it; she'd even intimated that Tom had met other young ladies out in the park and tried to frighten the wits out of them. Well, he'd better not now!

Lucy stared into the gathering darkness. She and the others

had heard the rumours. Candleton, at night, was always a frightening place but recently there had been more sinister stories and a sense of unease was growing among the household.

Lucy herself, not blessed with imagination, had experienced the frightening phenomena. Lights moving in the graveyard or down amongst the old ruins; footsteps out in the galleries when she knew no one was there. Now that strange priest had arrived. He looked no older than a boy in the company of his sharp-eyed sister.

Lucy heard a sound and froze. What was that? She strained her ears. Again the crack of a twig. Perhaps it was one of the gamekeepers? After all, Christmas was approaching and, although Lady Alice was a benevolent landlord, some of her tenants still regarded poaching as part of the seasonal activities.

'Who's there?'

Her voice echoed into the night. Lucy, cold, got up and stamped her feet.

'If you don't come soon, Tom Weston!' she hissed. 'I'm leaving!'

The night was still, the sky cloud-free. Lucy stared up. The stars were like gems on a black velvet cushion. Would Tom buy her a ring with a precious stone or even a locket where she could keep a tuft of his auburn hair? A dog howled, to be answered immediately by the old owl which hunted in the copse down near the mere. Lucy rubbed her hands together, glad she had brought her gloves. She would wait: she would count till fifty and do so slowly. If Tom hadn't arrived by the time she finished, well, there were others, like young Robert the farrier's son.

The snap of a twig stopped Lucy before she had even reached ten. She heard deep breathing. Someone was out there, hiding in the darkness, trying to frighten her.

'Tom Weston!' she called. 'Tom Weston, don't you do that!'

The only reply was a strange moaning sound followed by a low snigger. Lucy retreated deeper into the arbour. She forgot about counting now. She'd go straight back to the Hall.

She stepped out. The cold breeze buffeted her face; in the distance she could see the twinkling lights of the house. Lucy Gibson was frightened. It was so dark and so far to go! What happened if someone was there? She'd heard stories of men who preyed on innocent young maidens. Perhaps it would be best to wait until Tom came; moreover, she didn't wish to make a fool of herself. Lucy stepped back into the arbour, nestling in a corner. She heard slithering above her. Someone was up in the tree! She could hear the creak of the branches and the clatter of twigs on the arbour roof.

'Tom Weston!' she shouted. 'Tom, stop it!'

A low moaning sound. Lucy was now sure that Tom was playing one of his tricks. She was about to go out and confront him. She'd teach him a lesson! Then she heard a crack, a strange coughing sound. In her heart Lucy knew this was no foolery. Worse, an insistent tapping rattled the top of the arbour as if some imp there was trying to dig its way through. Lucy shook with fear. She dared not go out, it might jump on her. She started to scream.

Two gamekeepers at the far end of the park heard her cries for help and hurried across, stopping for a while to light their lanterns.

'It's coming from the great sycamore,' one of them observed. 'You know, the Hanging Tree!'

The younger gamekeeper, straining his eyes, agreed. He'd heard about the tree. According to local lore, it was where the Candleton lords, years earlier, had hanged felons and poachers.

He saw a flash of white in the arbour. They hurried on. In the pale light of the moon, as well as the glow from their lanterns, they saw Lucy hysterical with fear, hands to her face. She was still screaming.

'What on earth?' The young one raised his lantern and glimpsed what was hanging from the branch above the arbour. 'May the good Lord save us!' he breathed.

He ran into the arbour while his colleague, drawing his long hunting knife, climbed the sycamore. As soon as the younger man reached Lucy, the young chambermaid fainted into a dead swoon. The gamekeeper picked her up. He walked out and stared in horror at the corpse of young Tom Weston, now hanging by his neck, one end of the muffler tight round his throat, the other caught in the branches above.

Oliver woke up just before dawn. He moved his head and winced at the pain. The curtains had been drawn; faint chinks of sunlight came through the gaps. He pulled himself up. The pain in the back of his neck and shoulders made him gasp. Emma, sleeping in a chair before the fire, woke with a start.

'Welcome back,' she smiled. She gazed at her brother's pallid face. 'Before you ask, William says it's a bad crack to the head but you'll live.'

Oliver closed his eyes.

'Here, he left this for you.' Emma picked up a small glass of opiate and poured it between his lips. 'You'll feel tender and sore for a couple of days.'

'I'll feel tender and sore for a couple of months,' Oliver groaned.

'Well, you slept all yesterday. Tossing and turning you were.' Emma made him lean back against the pillows.

'I'm hungry,' Oliver murmured. 'My mouth is dry as sand.'

Emma went out to get some tea. By the time she returned, Oliver was fast asleep again. He remained so until late in the afternoon. When he awoke, the aches and pains had subsided. He felt more vigorous, clear-headed.

Dr Meddlecott came and pronounced him fit and well. He recommended a meal of grilled lamb cutlets, boiled potatoes and a small glass of red wine. Oliver ate this, pronouncing that he had never felt so hungry in his life.

Afterwards he dozed. It was dark when he awoke. He lay for a while listening to the sounds of the house. He heard voices on the stairs and Emma, accompanied by Lady Alice and the doctor, entered his bedchamber. For a while they teased and laughed with him but Oliver could see they were trying to hide something.

'What is it?' he asked sharply, pulling himself up on the bed.

'There's been another death,' Lady Alice replied. She pulled her chair closer into the pool of candlelight, her face wan and heavy-eyed from lack of sleep.

'It's one of the footmen, Tom Weston.' Meddlecott sat on the edge of the bed and felt Oliver's pulse. 'We don't know whether it was an accident, a silly escapade that went wrong or . . .'

'Or like Bennington's?' Oliver asked.

The doctor took his hand away. 'A young chambermaid, Lucy Gibson, much smitten by Weston, agreed to meet him beneath the old sycamore tree out in the park. Now, from what I can gather, Lucy was silly enough to go out. Tom, who was known for his practical jokes, tried to frighten her. He climbed the tree. He was wearing a long scarf or muffler. Apparently, one end caught on a branch. Tom slipped, it was like falling through a gallows trap. His body swung from the branch, his boots scuffing the top of the arbour. Lucy froze with fear and then became hysterical. God knows you can't blame her.'

'Two of my gamekeepers found them,' Lady Alice added. 'Poor Tom's neck was broken and it will be weeks before Lucy recovers her wits.'

Oliver crossed his arms. Panic seethed within him. He had never met anything like this.

'Can this happen?' Lady Alice asked as if she was reading his mind. 'Father, you were thrown downstairs. You could have been killed. Poor Bennington and Tom were ... I ...' She stammered. 'I don't think their deaths were accidents.'

'It can happen,' Oliver replied. 'It's nothing to do with ghosts or demons.' He glanced at Meddlecott. 'There's a lot of sense in what you said about the powers of the mind. I have shared stories of people who can move tables, levitate themselves and why should we dismiss them? Even in the Gospels Jesus said that He needed faith before He could cure someone and that, if we had real faith, we could uproot a tree. If that is true of life it must be more so about us after death.' He picked up the glass of water and sipped at it. 'Think of a mind, of an intellect, untrammelled by flesh and its limitations, intent on wreaking evil. So, yes, it can be done. Bennington could well have been pushed and the same is true of poor Tom Weston.'

'But you are a priest,' Meddlecott broke in crossly. 'You have the power of Christ. What about the angels and the saints?'

'What about them? The power of evil always has its day. This is no different.'

'Do you think we should give up?' Lady Alice asked.

'No, I don't.' Oliver tried to sound more confident. 'But I think we should approach it from a different perspective. The haunting is caused by a fount of evil, what I call the root. We must get to that.' Oliver drew himself up. 'And we must not give up faith or hope. We are dealing with wickedness which has battened on itself for centuries. I want to discover how, as well as why, it is now manifesting itself.'

'Is there anything I can do?' Lady Alice asked.

'Well, until I'm fit and ready to move around, and that should be soon, I would like the manuscripts brought up here. I don't want to lie looking at the ceiling. Boredom and ennui only assist the powers of darkness.'

Lady Alice got up. She came across and kissed Oliver lightly on the forehead. Meddlecott shook his hand, said he admired his courage, then left with Lady Alice.

'God help me,' Oliver whispered to Emma as soon as the door closed. 'They have more faith than I.'

Emma took from the pocket of her gown a small, cream-coloured piece of paper.

'You've had a letter from Thurston, the inspector you met at Seven Dials. You apparently did some good there.' Emma unfolded the letter. 'He's been talking to a Jesuit, says he wishes to enter the Church.'

'Thurston was a good officer.'

'Listen.' Emma opened the letter. ' "I would also like to say," ' she read, ' "that the authorities have acted swiftly over Benfleet's house in Seven Dials but money always speaks louder than good advice. The place has been cleaned, a lick of paint here and there, the rubbish removed but the owner insists that the property is too valuable to destroy and intends to let it out again." ' Emma looked up. 'Thurston sends you his good wishes. He still has memories of what he describes as "the most terrifying night of his life".'

'If the authorities are not careful,' Oliver snapped, 'there'll be more such nights.' He settled down on the bed. 'I'll pray for Thurston,' he murmured sleepily. 'I wish he was here.'

The next morning Emma, assisted by Stokes, brought documents and books up from the muniment room and library. Oliver made himself comfortable against the pillows. He felt more refreshed: his head still ached but he found he could concentrate.

Emma soon became absorbed in a file of letters belonging to Lady Thérèse Seaton, mistress of Candleton in the seventeenth century. She and Oliver went through them. Despite the two-hundred-year gap, they felt the deep poignancy of the disintegration of this young woman's mind as she slipped deeper and deeper into madness.

Some of the letters were lucid and clear, written to friends and relatives in France or at the Court of St James in London.

Others betrayed a sense of horror and impending doom.

'Listen to this one.' Emma made herself comfortable on the bed. 'It's dated 6th April 1679 and written to a physician, Dr George Vilyard, who had chambers in Piccadilly. "My dear George".' Emma glanced up. 'She had a good hand. The first paragraph is about the estates but the second is interesting: "The terrors of the night," ' Emma read on, ' "despite your good advice, still plague me. Candleton can be a lonely place. When the sun sets and the darkness falls, Hell spits out its most hideous horrors. I cannot sleep. At night the gallery echoes to the sound of footsteps. Time and again I rise but there's no one there. Nevertheless, I know she haunts me." ' Emma glanced up. 'The word "she" is heavily underlined.

' "The servants have seen things but they keep close counsel. Many now feign excuses for not coming up to the Hall: illness, the need to make a journey or inclement weather. Sometimes I am alone. I have asked for help but who believes me? The only assistance I get is from a wine goblet or a jar of laudanum. Last night was the worst. I went down to the Spanish Chamber. A ghastly place, that red leather deadens all sound! I opened the casement window and the moonlight bathed it in a silver glow. I wish she'd come! I want to confront her, drive her out of this place! Instead I saw a hideous sight, a vision from the past.

' "I was sitting by the table. I didn't know whether I was asleep or awake when a young man appeared in the room. He was dressed in a hood and cloak and played nervously with the hilt of a dagger strapped to his belt. He was travel-stained and weary. I saw her, Isabella, Queen of the Night! She gave this young man a goblet. He died before my eyes in dreadful agony and there was nothing I could do. I was so terrified I dare not move but sat as if imprisoned on the spot. Eventually, as on other nights, I climbed back to my chambers and slept fitfully till daybreak." '

Emma put the letter down. 'The rest is general news about her health, her desire to escape from here.'

'This is not like any place I have ever visited,' Oliver mused. 'Candleton is trapped in time. This Isabella was not what she claimed to be.'

'What do you mean?'

Oliver pulled himself up. 'People do evil things. They commit dreadful acts. The king at the time, Richard III, had his rivals executed. In a sense, you can see the logic of his actions: he was frightened and he was vulnerable. Lady Isabella was different. She struck out against anyone who might frustrate her ambitions.'

'But we have no proof of that?'

'No, but I intend to find it. I believe Lady Isabella Seaton was a terrible murderess. The author of hideous horrors. Worse, she may have practiced the black arts. In the fifteenth century, sorcery and witchcraft in England reached sophisticated levels, often used against enemies or political opponents.' He paused. 'Isabella Seaton may have sold her soul.'

'For what?'

'For Candleton. Just think, Emma! Young and spoilt when she came here, Isabella grew obsessed with the place. It becomes her whole reason for living: no God, no morality, no friends, only her desire to possess, to keep Candleton for herself, whatever the odds.

'Death is like birth. Once we are gone,' he caught Emma's gaze, 'for most people it's a new beginning, they do not want to come back. Lady Isabella was, is, different, because she still refuses to relinquish Candleton.'

They went back to their searches. Now and again Emma would interrupt with further scraps of information about poor Lady Thérèse. Oliver concentrated on those documents from the time when Lady Isabella held power of life and death over Candleton and all who lived there.

They worked on through until dark. Oliver ate a light supper in his room, said his office and spent an untroubled night. The following morning he began again. Lady Alice and Dr Meddlecott came up to visit him. Stokes brought some small file cards. Oliver, using a special writing tray, wrote his conclusions out on them.

By evening he felt stronger and, though his neck and arms ached, he insisted on getting up. He washed, dressed and went down to the Spanish Chamber. For a long while he studied the tapestry by the light of a candle, moving slowly from one scene to the next.

The chamber was silent as the grave. Oliver found his gaze distracted, pulled by the face in the portrait next to the glass. At times, he thought someone was standing behind him but, when he looked, there was nothing.

At last he was finished and joined the rest for supper in the small dining room. For most of the meal they chattered about the weather and what they would do at Christmas. Lady Alice gave Oliver warning glances. The priest realised the servants were only too willing to stay and eavesdrop. He sensed a change of mood among them. The household was deeply disturbed by Weston's death and Lucy's breakdown. Few would meet his eye and there were no smiles for him and Emma.

Once supper was over and Stokes had shooed the servants out, Oliver got to his feet to ease the cramp: he reassured the doctor that the pain in his head had now subsided.

'Nothing but a dull ache in my neck,' he declared. 'And that will go. But listen, I want to tell you about Lady Isabella.'

He paused. A rose bush outside one of the windows shook in the brisk night winds, its spidery branches lashing the paned glass. Oliver went and opened the window. The cold night air chilled the sweat on his brow; although he did not tell his companions, the priest sensed that the Presence had also come to listen, to mock his puny efforts. He slammed the window shut and walked back.

'Lady Isabella Seaton,' he began, 'married Sir Henry when she was very young. He indulged her. She fell in love with this place and wanted to possess it. Events outside Candleton helped her – the war between the Houses of York and Tudor. Sir Henry conceived what he thought was a clever, subtle strategy. He and one of his sons would fight for King Richard. His other son Benedict would join kinsman Alain Montague and support the invader Henry Tudor.'

Oliver paused, resting his hand on the back of his chair. 'Now I can only guess what happened. Lady Isabella supported this scheme but secretly devised her own. Sir Henry was old. Lord Montague, I suspect, was a young, hot-eyed courtier who had fallen deeply in love with his old kinsman's wife.'

'You've found proof of this?' Meddlecott interjected.

'Yes, to a certain extent I have but I'll show you that later. Let me give you the story as I think it happened.'

'Priest!' The word was spoken in a hoarse, hissing whisper.

Oliver stared around. The others apparently hadn't heard it and sat waiting for him to continue.

'Clever priest, have you not learnt your lesson?'

Oliver felt his hands shake. He breathed in, closed his eyes and muttered a short prayer.

'Arthur sends his good wishes and greetings! He's with Master Benfleet now. You know what Master Benfleet liked to do with small boys?'

Oliver gripped the back of his chair. 'You're a liar!' he whispered. 'In Jesus' name, leave me alone!'

'Oliver, are you all right?' Emma half rose from her chair.

'Yes, Emma.' He felt a little nauseous and sat down. 'I'll tell you this honestly,' he said much louder than he intended. 'And I ask Christ and His angels to witness that I speak the truth.'

The clamour inside his head faded though he could still hear it, as if some child stood in a shadowy corner and whispered and giggled.

'As I've said, Lord Montague and Lady Isabella became the best of friends, perhaps even lovers. When civil war broke out in the summer of 1485, Ralph Seaton went with Lord Montague. He was killed, probably murdered by Alain during the battle. Meanwhile, on the Yorkist side Sir Henry had been taken prisoner. He probably expected Montague to intervene. His kinsman did, but not as they had planned: Alain may have insinuated that Sir Henry Seaton had been a fervent Yorkist and, in the heat of battle, he was hanged out of hand.

'His corpse was left on a gibbet. Lady Isabella didn't want it back. Now, it was rare in medieval times for a corpse to be stolen. I suspect she or Lord Montague arranged for it to be despatched into some marsh or morass.'

'And Benedict?' Lady Alice asked. She sat gripping the table edge: Oliver suspected she, too, was quietly being harassed by the Presence which controlled this Hall.

'Oh, he fled the battlefield. Perhaps he suspected all was not well. He returned to Candleton by secret routes. Lady Isabella was waiting: he came by night but, instead of being given succour, he was quietly poisoned. Lady Isabella intended to make a clean sweep. After all he was a rebel, a fugitive from royal justice. She killed him and his remains probably lie somewhere in the lake or the grounds of Candleton Hall.

'Once all three were disposed of, Lady Isabella came into her own. Thanks to Montague's influence, as well as the Tudor's desire not to alienate more than he should, Lady Isabella could depict herself as a loyal supporter of the new monarch. For a while she acted the grieving widow, the stepmother, bereft of her two sons, but secretly she must have laughed at the way she played her game. Lord Montague, naturally, would demand his share of the reward: Isabella's body, marriage and a share in the Seaton wealth. Of course she'd murdered once, so it was easy to do it again. Lord Alain met with a fatal accident.

'After that, Lady Isabella eventually emerged as the *grande dame* of the Norfolk countryside. If she wanted a lover she would take one. Above all, she had Candleton.'

Oliver felt the back of his neck poked as if someone had jabbed with their fingers, making the dull ache flare into biting pain. He winced and muttered a prayer, shaking his head at Emma's worried expression.

'You mentioned proof,' Lady Alice said.

'Yes, yes, I did. First, it's in the manuscripts. Isn't it strange that all the men associated with Lady Isabella, men who could threaten her claim on Candleton, met violent and bloody deaths?'

'As you will!' The whisper echoed in his brain. 'You and your mealy-mouthed sister!'

'Proof is also there,' Oliver continued remorselessly, 'of Lady Isabella's other nefarious activities. They appear innocent enough: payments made to an old woman from the village, Petronella. According to the records, this woman had a reputation for being a witch, of dabbling in the black arts. In 1484 Sir Henry received a petition from the parish of Candleton levelling serious accusations against Petronella. However, nothing seems to have come of it. Now, in the household accounts, under gifts given at Easter and Christmas, Petronella is listed as one of those receiving payments and tokens from Lady Isabella.'

'Wouldn't that have made her suspect?'

'No, no, Lady Isabella could act the lady of the manor, having pity on some poor unfortunate. Other gifts were made. Moreover, once Sir Henry left to join Richard's forces in the early summer of 1485, Petronella became a frequent visitor to the manor, often by night. We know that because payments were made to servants "for carrying torches in bringing Petronella to Candleton".'

Oliver paused and stared down at the window now being lashed by the branches of the rose bush, an ominous clatter, as if someone were drumming with their fingers, desperate to get in.

'At the same time, although her husband had left for war,' Oliver continued. 'Lady Isabella arranged for special building work to be done. In the document it's called "*pro secreta camera*": Wulfstan, a carpenter and local mason, was hired.'

'What does that tell us?' Meddlecott asked nervously, filling his port glass then rubbing his hands at the growing coldness in the room.

'The phrase means,' Oliver replied, 'that Isabella had a secret chamber built at Candleton.'

'There are stories about that,' Lady Alice interrupted. 'But no one has ever found it. Do the manuscripts give any clue?'

'Very little, except considerable building materials were bought. By 14th August 1485 this secret work was completed. After that there are no further references to Petronella: she seems to have vanished from the face of the earth!'

'What about Wulfstan?' Emma asked. 'Any local builder or mason would chatter about what he was doing.'

'Oh, no, Lady Isabella took care of Wulfstan. He apparently stayed in the manor while he did the building work. He never left alive. There's an entry in the household book, just before Michaelmas 1485, for a Mass to be said for the repose of the soul of Wulfstan the mason. Apparently he met with an accident when working at the Hall.'

'Murdered?' Emma asked.

'Undoubtedly, to keep his mouth shut. I suspect the same fate befell Petronella. Lady Isabella used both of them to build a secret room: her temple to the demons. They couldn't be left to chatter and gossip. I wonder if their souls are also doomed to haunt Candleton?'

Oliver got up and walked towards the fire. This house, he

thought, must be thronged with ghosts. Only a few nights ago he had been hurled down the stairs, now he was experiencing different phenomena: the room growing colder, those dreadful whispers which seared his consciousness, the ominous rapping on the window. Yet he had been allowed to tell his story. He stretched his hands out, oblivious to the others staring at him curiously from the table.

'I have said enough,' he remarked quietly. 'The shadows are gathering. Perhaps it's best if I show you the proof in the full light of day.'

Chapter 9

Lady Alice sat in her bedchamber. Ruth, standing behind her, combed her long hair. Lady Alice toyed with the bow of her nightgown. She stared through the mirror and glimpsed the full expanse of her majestic four-poster bed. She rubbed her arms.

'Madam feels cold?'

Lady Alice smiled. 'More the weather than anything, Ruth.'

She shook her head and tied back her hair with a ribbon. The gesture reminded her of sweeter days, sitting here, practising how her hair should hang. Now it was all gone; Sir Thomas, her love for him nothing more than a sham! As if in response, her belly contracted in pain. Alice smiled. The child was proving her wrong. She must remember that and not let the darkness into her soul.

She glanced up. Ruth stood waiting for Lady Alice to speak, perhaps discuss what had really happened to poor Tom and Lucy.

The corpse had been taken down to Candleton. The coroner would, once again, sit and rule that Tom, like Bennington, had suffered a dreadful accident. Those beneath the stairs knew differently. Horrors were loose at Candleton and many blamed that interfering priest.

Lady Alice glanced in the mirror. Ruth was watching her strangely.

'I think that will be enough, Ruth,' she said. 'You may retire for the night.'

Ruth bobbed a curtsey then went and folded back the sheets on the bed.

'Goodnight, ma'am!'

'Goodnight, Ruth. If I need you, I'll call.'

Lady Alice waited until the maid closed the door then went to stand at the window. The wind was still blowing strong. Clouds scurried across the night sky. She could make out the outlines of the trees, their bare branches bending under the force of the strengthening wind.

Lady Alice felt frightened and trapped. On the one hand Father Oliver was a good priest, stubborn, dedicated to the task in hand but Lady Alice wondered if she had opened Pandora's Box. What happened if the haunting could not be exorcised? What if she herself had released forces which strengthened the malevolence seeping through Candleton Hall? In a way, she could accept the ghostly footsteps at night, the ominous rappings, even that hideous dark shape. But what about her own secrets? What if Father Oliver, or his sharp-witted sister, began to question the ghosts which haunted her own mind and soul?

Lady Alice sighed and returned to the stool before the mirror. She sat with her back to it so she would not be forced to confront herself.

She trusted Dr William, yet the physician was much smitten by Emma Grafeld. What if he began to talk? Let slip her secrets? Would Father Oliver ask to hear her confession? Examine her guilt? She closed her eyes: that was one ghost the priest must not see! Sir Thomas, on his horse, that deep-bowled cup in his hands.

In her mind's eye, Lady Alice imagined the hounds streaming across the fields. Sir Thomas, determined to be first, his horse gathering speed, legs coming together for the vault which would carry it across the hedge but then the stumble. Sir Thomas had been hurtled up into the air, and those present even claimed they could hear the crack of his neck as he fell. How everyone had gathered round to comfort her in her grieving yet, even then, she had stared surreptitiously across the drawing room and seen Ralph Mowbray gazing intently at her. Sin was not only the act but the thought.

Lady Alice sat up, breathing in deeply. She turned to take the hair brush from the dressing table and stared in horror at the reflection in the mirror. It was no longer herself. The woman was draped in black, and the wimple around the face only accentuated her yellowing skin! The sharp nose, harsh mouth and that malevolent, glaring stare . . .

Father Oliver lay on his side in bed, the blankets pulled up. He had finished the Divine Office and retired immediately, nestling deep down in the warmth. At first his mind had been filled with jarring, clashing images. He did not wish to admit it but he was afraid. He still felt unprepared, lacking in confidence at what he had to confront.

Oliver slipped into a deep sleep full of dreams from the past: his parents' cottage in Sussex; Arthur waiting under the oak tree, the sun dappling the fields; Emma chasing him; sitting in that parlour staring in amazement at Arthur who was speaking to him softly, reassuring him. Other images followed: his years of study in Valladolid; hauntings, eerie experiences; that terrifying exorcism in the candle-lit sanctuary of Valladolid's great gothic cathedral. Oliver drifted on, then he awoke. Someone was calling his name.

'Oliver, Oliver, Oliver!'

Just like Arthur used to, when his elder brother hid and Oliver couldn't find him. He tried to ignore it, pulling the blankets more firmly under his chin. He dismissed it as part of a dream, not wanting to consider the sinister influences curling their way around this haunted Hall.

'Oliver! Oliver! Oliver!'

In exasperation the priest rolled over and sat on the edge of the bed. He recoiled in horror. Coming out of the wall, hands extended, dressed in white from head to toe, the thin gauze veil barely concealing her cruel, powerful face was his adversary, Lady Isabella, lips moving, mimicking Arthur's voice.

Oliver leapt from the bed. He crouched in terror, not daring to look as his sweat-soaked fingers fumbled with the tinder box. At last the candle wick caught the flame. Oliver moved across to the table and lit some more. Only then, repeating a prayer, did he turn and look. The horrid apparition had disappeared. The room was empty, and only the curtains moved faintly as the wind pierced the cracks and vents in the windows.

Oliver went on his knees. He joined his hands and intoned verses from the psalms until at last he controlled his fear. Then he went to the door and opened it. The gallery outside was dark, cold and empty. He walked back into the room; a sense of malevolence, of being secretly watched, made him uneasy. He did not want to react, to give way to the hysteria bubbling inside him. Oliver knew from his training as an exorcist how these were signs of weakness, a lack of faith and hope in God's help.

For a while he sat in a chair leafing through a picture book which described the Norfolk Broads. Only when he felt a calm did he blow out the candles and climb back into bed. He wondered if Emma were safe but she would surely have roused him and, if he sent to see her, she would only become fearful.

Oliver pondered which tactics he should adopt. He was following the right course, collecting information, determined to remedy wrongs done. He would prepare himself thoroughly before another exorcism. He kept thinking about Lady Alice's face, the way she gripped the tablecloth: sooner or later he must confront her, ask why these hauntings had begun now? Were they connected to her late husband's death?

Oliver rolled over to one side and, half muttering a prayer, drifted off to sleep while the hate-filled Presence in the shadows seethed with malice and also watched and waited.

Oliver celebrated Mass late the next morning. Afterwards, he, Lady Alice, Emma and Dr Meddlecott breakfasted on bacon, toast, muffins, scrambled eggs and sausages. Lady Alice nibbled at her food. Oliver ate heartily enough; the pain at the back of his neck had gone. He realised that what had happened last night was ghostly bullying, a common experience for exorcists. Time and again in every manual, in every instruction Oliver had been given, he had been warned of such phenomena. The experts, basing their opinions on the Gospels, demonstrated how, when confronted by an exorcist, the Spirits of the Air often exhibited terrifying manifestations to frighten, humiliate and eventually beat down.

Oliver ruefully admitted to himself that he had nearly given way to such a temptation. Now he felt angry, not only at the hurt caused but at the malicious insolence of being baited with the voice of his dead brother.

Oliver only hoped that Lady Alice could be helped. He admired her courage and knew that, despite her protestations, she too must be baited and frightened like the seventeenth-century Lady Thérèse who lost her mind and wits. He envied Emma and Dr Meddlecott. They sat talking about the dangers of serving abroad and the lack of good medical practitioners in the army. Now and again Emma would glance sideways and study her brother: he was troubled and distressed but Oliver hated being fussed, particularly in the presence of others.

After he had served himself a second helping, the doctor announced that he must return to Candleton to see his patients.

'But last night you mentioned proof,' he added, 'about Lady Isabella? Oh, by the way,' the doctor dabbed his mouth with his napkin, 'you heard voices last night didn't you? When you were speaking to us at dinner?'

'I don't like the way you are looking at me,' Oliver joked. 'Next thing I know, a sealed carriage will be rolling up to whisk me off to Bedlam.'

Emma laughed but Dr Meddlecott shook his head.

'That's why you stopped, wasn't it?' he insisted.

'Yes, yes, it was. And yet,' Oliver continued, 'we must not be frightened of them.' He stared down the table at Lady Alice. 'They are tricks, pin-pricks, part of the haunting process. You read stories where ghosts tend to appear and disappear at will.' He smiled. 'And that happens. I read a very famous story in *The Times*, how a guard at the Tower of London saw a ghostly figure, attacked it with his bayonet and then called out the guard. Such apparitions are not really ghosts. They are elementals, puffs of smoke from a fire long gone out.'

'But this is different, unique.' Lady Alice spoke harshly.

'Yes it is. We are confronted by a thinking, free-willed, malevolent presence which probably holds others in thrall. So far we have been frightened. But that's because we frighten it. Now, I want to show you the proof.'

He led them out of the dining room, up the stairs and along the galleries to the Spanish Chamber.

When they entered, Oliver immediately sensed a presence, not Lady Isabella's. This was quieter, sad.

'Where's this proof then?' Meddlecott asked, eager to break the silence.

'It's here.' Oliver led them over to the tapestry behind the glass. 'What do you see there?'

Meddlecott perched his spectacles on the end of his nose. He studied the tapestry as if he were inspecting a bandage in a hospital. Emma caught Oliver's gaze and winked.

'God knows,' the doctor declared. 'Strange symbols, demons. The embroidery is very good.'

'It was sewn by Mathilda Seaton,' Oliver explained. 'The sort of tapestry to hang in a solar or even a church. The motif is quite common, reminiscent of some of the drawings of Hieronymous Bosch, phantasms, exotic creatures.'

'But there's more, isn't there?' Lady Alice asked. 'I've known that since I came here.'

'Yes there is. In different parts of the tapestry are scenes which you can recognise: look at the gatehouse.'

'Why that's Candleton!' Emma exclaimed. 'Not immediately recognisable but it's the manor house. And who's that?' She pointed further along to where a man, dressed in a cloak and holding a knife, was hurrying towards it.

'I suspect that's Benedict Seaton,' Oliver replied. 'Fleeing back after the battle of Bosworth.'

'But where's the proof that he was killed?' Lady Alice asked.

'Ah, that's the beauty of this tapestry. The house is down here but, see the opposite far corner, amongst that vine grove?'

They all stood on tiptoe. Mathilda had embroidered a beautiful creeping vine: the green of its stem was still vivid, the grapes were a full purple. In the centre of its tendrils, the man they had glimpsed further down was now with a woman, dressed like a nun, who was pouring wine into his mouth.

'Now, follow the tendrils down into the main branch of the vine. It goes right along the tapestry, look at the bottom.'

Emma did so and gasped: the man, dressed in the cloak and hood, lay out on the grounds, hands together like a corpse dressed for burial.

'It's only guesswork,' Oliver said. 'However, over here, on one side of the tapestry, we have an army. A scene which can be found in any Book of Hours. There are the soldiers with helmets and pikes, indistinguishable one from the other. But study them carefully. Dr Meddlecott, Hippocrates said a good physician must be a keen observer.' Oliver put down his own spectacles. 'What's so singular about this scene?'

Meddlecott crouched down. He was about to give up when he tapped at the glass. 'None of the soldiers carry insignia except one, a small eagle on his helm.'

'The Seaton emblem,' Emma offered.

'Goodness!' the doctor exclaimed. 'You can't see it at first but there's another man driving a small dagger into his neck.

You would miss it unless you really studied it closely.'

'Lord Montague killing Ralph Seaton. Now, across the tapestry,' Oliver explained, 'we have a forest: the soldiers are dressed the very same as the ones we have just studied, they are hanging a man.'

'Sir Henry,' Lady Alice whispered. 'But there's no Seaton emblem?'

'Yes, but look above the trees. What do you see? An eagle flying against the sun. Now, in popular medieval lore, that was taken as a sign for St John. I suspect here it stands for the Seaton eagle, or Sir Henry's soul flying to God.'

'There's one scene I remember.' Lady Alice now stood back and the others followed. 'Yes there it is.' She pointed to a man falling off a horse. The animal's legs were caught in a privet and the rider was being pitched forward.

'That, I suspect,' Oliver said, 'is Lord Alain Montague.'

'The whole tapestry,' Emma exclaimed, 'is a confession.'

'I think so,' Oliver replied. 'And very cleverly done. There are some images I don't understand. I'd like to know what this refers to?' He pointed to the top of the tapestry. 'See, it's in Latin, "*per Hispaniam*", "through Spain". And, at the bottom, "*ad secreta*", "to the secrets". And this man over here.' He pointed to a figure of a man kneeling, hands joined, dressed in the brown garb of a friar. This broke Oliver's dream of lying in the churchyard. 'It could well be the chaplain,' he added. 'Peter Rivers.'

'But Mathilda was simple-minded,' Lady Alice said.

'No,' Dr Meddlecott replied. 'They might have thought that, and perhaps it was a mental illness which came and went. Whatever, Mathilda was a consummate artist and a keen observer of what was going on around her.'

'Mathilda Seaton,' Oliver declared, 'was a sharp-eyed, very astute woman. Lady Isabella, in her arrogance, did not see her as an enemy but Mathilda lived to be an old woman. Because of her handicap, whatever it was, she was safe from Isabella's venom. She knew she could not confront her stepmother: instead, she wove her secrets into this tapestry, a sort of confession.'

'But, if she was astute?' Emma asked. 'Why didn't she confront Lady Isabella publicly?'

'Who would believe her?'

'She must have hated Isabella.'

Emma pointed to the different scenes of the tapestry. She wished she could take the glass away and stroke the colours, still quite brilliant in places, the blues, reds and golds. This was part of a human soul. A woman who had suffered, witnessed horrible evil but had been powerless to do anything about it.

Oliver crouched down. 'It's fascinating,' he said. 'One thing is missing: Mathilda died after Lady Isabella but there appears to be no reference to her stepmother's mysterious disappearance.'

He got to his feet and moved to the portrait, staring at it to memorise every detail. Even though the painting had been done over three hundred years earlier, Oliver caught the power of this formidable woman, the strength in those shrewd, calculating eyes, the set of the lips and chin. A lady of indomitable will who had turned to evil.

'You said Lady Isabella was involved in black magic?' Meddlecott asked. 'Is that why Mathilda had those scenes of Hell and devils woven all over the tapestry?'

'I think so,' Oliver replied. 'And that's why I'd love to understand the manuscript I found in the muniment room. In that, I'm sure, lies the answer to all this but it's written in an obscure cipher. I could send it to London?'

'Is it so hard to translate?' Lady Alice asked.

'Once we find the key, it'll be as easy as turning a well-oiled lock but, with such ciphers, we could search for years.'

Lady Alice jumped as the window casement behind her

slammed shut. The sound was like a crack, as if they were being reminded of where they were and whom they were discussing. She went to look out at the steel-grey sky.

'It's going to snow,' she murmured.

Oliver joined Lady Alice at the window. Already the first few white flakes were falling, melting immediately as they landed on the sill outside.

'I'd like to walk around,' he said. 'Just by myself.'

'You are sure?' Lady Alice asked him. 'Stokes or one of us could join you.'

'No,' Oliver replied absentmindedly.

He went down the stairs and out through the main door. Halfway across the bridge he stopped and stared down at the moat. The water was beginning to freeze. Oliver buttoned his coat up, pulling up the lapels. He gazed around. Candleton didn't look so lovely in the grip of winter. Across the parkland, the black trees lifted their branches to the sky. They looked like demons, their frozen arms raised in supplication.

'Careful, careful!' he murmured to himself. 'You have enough enemies, Grafeld, without letting your imagination run riot.'

He glanced up at the great gatehouse and the Seaton escutcheon emblazoned above it. His gaze moved along the front of the house, where a movement caught his eye. A figure was standing in one of the great bay windows looking down at him. Oliver blinked and stared again. Lady Isabella! She was dressed in widow's weeds, her white face framed by a black wimple. Even from where he stood Oliver sensed her malicious intent. He refused to flinch or lower his eyes.

'Oliver! Oliver!'

Emma came out through the archway holding his cane, gloves and hat.

'What are you staring at?' she exclaimed.

Oliver looked up at the window, but the face had gone.

'You won't be too long will you?'

'A short walk only.'

He put on the gloves and hat, thanked her and, swinging the cane, walked across the bridge into the parkland.

Oliver found the silence was unnerving. The death of the young footman and Lucy's well-founded hysteria had only deepened the gloom at Candleton. Now and again he met the occasional servant. Oliver greeted them cheerfully but they either forced a smile and hurried on or looked darkly at him. Oliver sighed. To the people of Candleton, ghosts and eerie occurrences were bad enough but many would also remember the strange tales about the Catholic Church and, perhaps, were not as welcoming as he would like.

Oliver was going around to the back of the Hall when he stopped, fingers to his lips. Perhaps he should visit the tree where the tragedy had occurred?

He walked across the parkland. The ground was hard under foot and the snow was falling more thickly. Oliver felt as if he was out on some moor. Now and again he would pause and glance back at the manor house for reassurance. From the conversation at breakfast he'd learnt the tree where Tom Weston had died was a sycamore with a small wooden arbour built against its trunk.

As he passed the great oak trees, he remembered Christmases in Sussex. He, Emma and Arthur would love to walk in the snow-covered fields, trying to distinguish the different animal tracks. Oliver passed a small copse and stopped. A roe deer stood there, one leg slightly raised. Oliver recalled the words of the psalm: 'I search for thee oh Lord, as a deer thirsts for clear water.'

He stood admiring its grace and glossy, white-spotted colouring. The roe deer stared back.

'You are beautiful,' Oliver told it.

The deer tossed its head up and disappeared back into the

thickets. Oliver continued walking. He found the sycamore and went inside the small arbour. The girl had left one of her black mittens and a small stick she must have been shredding. The priest stepped outside and looked up at the interweaving branches of the tree. In summer it would be a beautiful sight, a glorious greenness, but now it looked like a scaffold. Oliver examined the trunk above the arbour. It must have been easy to climb, especially for a young man intent on mischief. He could see how in the dark, a scarf might catch the branches, which would be slippery. He crossed himself. Yet was it an accident? He glanced over his shoulder back at the house. He was distracted by a rabbit loping across the grass looking for any fresh shoots; a crow burst out of the branches of the tree and circled, calling raucously.

It was no accident, Oliver concluded. That young man had been pushed, frightened, as the Presence made its power felt. Such malignancy would resent such love, such innocent play.

The priest walked back towards the house and turned right, following the small trackway down through the lych gate. Inside the cemetery Oliver paused as he recalled his own dream. The church door was open. He went inside and bolted it behind him.

A small stove placed at the back of the church provided some warmth. Oliver went into the sanctuary, lit the candles on the altar, then went behind it. He could see where Bennington had been working, dressing the stone. He crossed to the marble sarcophagus. Oliver inspected this carefully, tapping at it, beating his heel against the flagstones. Was Lady Isabella's secret chamber here, beneath the church? Was that why she had built this memorial? Or was it just an empty symbol of her evil hypocrisy? He could find nothing amiss and, taking one of the candles, went down the steps into the crypt. He read the different inscriptions on the tombs: those from the previous century, flowery, often declaiming in poor Latin verse the achievements of the different Seatons and their families. Deeper in the darkness, he came across the medieval tombs, including Mathilda Seaton's with the dates of her birth and death and a simple inscription, '*O Jesus miserere!*' carved beneath.

Oliver went deeper into the crypt. At last, in the far corner, he came across the tomb of Peter Rivers the chaplain, no more than a stone plinth raised from the floor. The sheet of carved brass overlaying it had faded. Oliver crouched down. He could make out the chaplain's name, the date of his death and then some curious symbols. Oliver moved the candle: it was a series of letters. He felt inside his coat, took out a pencil and a small notebook and carefully copied the letters down: IND: EOE: GOC: ONF: IDO.

When he had finished Oliver put his spectacles on, sat with his back to the wall and stared down at the jumble of meaningless words. He was sure this was the same code used in the document he had found. The chaplain must have insisted that this cipher be on his tomb. Oliver put the notebook away.

'Did you mean me to find it?' he asked the darkness.

As if in answer the door to the crypt slammed shut and the candle flame guttered out. Oliver got to his feet. The crypt had grown much colder. He plucked the rosary beads from his pocket and wound them round his hand as he slowly edged his way forward.

'Help me!' The words came in a whisper.

Oliver turned to face where the voice had come from.

'Help me!' The tone was stronger, more demanding.

Oliver waited: feet apart, he forced himself to relax. No other phenomena or manifestations appeared, apart from the clinging coldness and his own sense of unease. As he waited the air grew warmer; the sweet, herbal smell of lavender and thyme filled the crypt. The fragrance awoke memories of his mother's kitchen and the jars which stood on the shelves above the sink.

'This is hallowed ground!' he called out. 'Why are you here? Where are you from? What is your name?'

'Help me!'

Oliver turned as if to go away. 'I cannot help you,' he called out.

'Pray!' the voice shouted. 'Say Masses in reparation, for peace and repose!'

'For whose souls?'

'For all of us!'

'Who are all of you?'

'Those still held by her. We cannot move on. We see the light but her will holds us back. In life,' the voice added wearily, 'so in death.'

Oliver crossed himself. 'By what name are you called?'

'Mathilda, Mathilda Seaton.'

'Why are you here?'

'For a terrible sin.'

'What sin?'

'Only in confession.'

'I am a priest.'

'But you cannot hear my confession. All we can do is ask for help.'

Oliver peered into the darkness. He glimpsed it, like a grey pillar of smoke, an indistinguishable shape.

'Why can't you move on?' Oliver insisted.

'Why can't you help me?' the voice pleaded. 'The evil must be purged by the living. That is why we must have Masses. Masses in the secret place.'

'What secret place? Where is it?'

'You must discover that yourself,' the voice added wearily. The smell of lavender and thyme grew stronger.

'I can pray for you,' Oliver said. 'I shall have Masses offered up but there is great evil here.'

'There always has been.' The reply was sharp. 'Like a rotting tree with deep roots.'

'How do I know you are not tricking me?' Oliver felt like a child asking questions in some game.

'No trickery here.' The reply was again sharp. 'Roots must be dug up. Evil resolved, reparation made, Masses said.' The voice began to fade.

Oliver's skin prickled with cold sweat. The smell of lavender and thyme, sweet and lingering, abruptly disappeared. Something else was in the crypt, loathsome and dark like a huge shadow racing across a field to blot out the sunlight.

Oliver heard a sharp hiss and looked around. He fumbled in his pocket for the matches but he was shoved as someone crashed into him. He went staggering back against the wall, then steadied himself as terrible screams echoed through the crypt.

'Mercy! Mistress, mercy!'

'As guilty as I am!' The voice was hoarse.

Oliver did not wait any longer. Stumbling and falling, he ran along the crypt, dropping the candlestick. He reached the steps and climbed up, muttering the word 'Jesus' a number of times. He flung himself at the door. It was unlocked. Oliver staggered into the church. Behind him the crypt had fallen silent. No sound, nothing. Oliver slammed the door shut and walked into the sanctuary. He knelt on the altar steps and stared up at the winking red sanctuary lamp.

He regretted leaving the crypt, running like a coward. He almost wished the Presence would come here. Oliver looked up at the altar and reached his decision.

Chapter 10

Oliver returned to the muniment room. Emma joined him a short while later.

'I won't celebrate a Mass today,' Oliver declared. 'Tomorrow afternoon, if Lady Alice is agreeable, I would like to visit that island then say a special Mass afterwards.' He took off his coat. 'Have you found anything else?'

Emma tapped the volume. 'This is a history compiled by a Seaton at the turn of the century. Apparently Candleton Hall has always provoked an interest in its history from its occupants. This includes the usual list of Seaton achievements both here or abroad: children born; the price of crops; the effect of war; the exploits of Seatons who served in the army or navy. However, there's something I must investigate further.' She opened the volume and a small cloud of dust rose from the pages. She smiled at Oliver. 'History's interesting, not only what it says but what it omits.'

Oliver let her read on. He took out his notebook and stared at the letters he had copied down from the chaplain's tomb.

The day wore on. Stokes brought in more candles, cups of steaming hot chocolate and some biscuits; he built up the fire and left. Oliver and Emma worked on, the silence only broken by the chiming of the clock which echoed like the peals of a bell through the muniment room.

Oliver realised that the inscription on the tomb was a key to the cipher. He played about with it; Emma got up and came round to ask what he was doing, but Oliver muttered that he wished he knew and returned to his doodling.

Emma went in and out of the library bringing various

volumes from the shelves. Now and again she'd go to the different chests or stand peering at the shelves, muttering under her breath.

'What's the matter?' Oliver asked crossly.

'Nothing.'

'I beg your pardon?'

'Nothing.' Emma smiled. 'That is the problem. According to the family history,' she explained, 'Candleton Hall was fairly quiet after the death of Lady Thérèse. Oh, phenomena were described, along with legends and stories, but nothing remarkable.

'In the 1760s Sir Maurice Seaton married a young noble-woman from Northumberland, Margaret Clifford. Again a happy marriage and that's when the mystery begins again. Sir Maurice's exploits, both as a farmer and as a soldier fighting in America, are quite accurately described, as are the early years of Lady Margaret's marriage and the children she bore. But then there's a complete and utter silence. Lady Margaret died in 1805 but the events between 1790 and that date are totally omitted. It is almost as if she died fifteen years earlier!'

'And so you went looking?'

'Yes and it doesn't make very pleasant reading. From about 1787 England was constantly at war either in America or against the French. Sir Maurice was absent from the Hall for considerable periods of time so Lady Margaret was entrusted with his affairs and the management of the estate. According to letters and documents that I have studied,' Emma raised her eyes heavenwards, 'mercifully the writing is easier to decipher now, this lovely Northumberland lass transformed into a veritable virago. While her husband was absent, or so rumour has it, she had liaisons with different men. She rode roughshod over the rights of the tenants and, if some of the gossip is to be believed, even hunted her poor tenants as other people do a fox!'

'How extraordinary.' Oliver sat back in the chair.

'It was a time of unrest,' Emma continued. 'Revolutionary doctrines swept England from America and France and the power of the printing press made itself felt. Apparently local feeling ran so strong, anonymous hand-bills were produced accusing Lady Margaret of the most devilish crimes.' Emma picked up one yellowing manuscript. 'According to this, matters became worse after Sir Maurice had been killed fighting the French in the Low Countries. Lady Margaret drove out the local vicar. When a deputation of peasants came to the Hall to protest, she had them horse-whipped from the bridge to the lodge gates.'

'Continue.'

'Eventually, even the local MP became involved. Petitions were presented in the House of Commons. Other local landlords begged Lady Margaret to show her tenants more compassion and mercy but to no avail. Her eldest son, when he reached sixteen, even consulted lawyers. Other kinsfolk became involved but nothing could be done.'

Oliver listened intently. 'I wonder . . .' he murmured.

'What?' Emma asked.

'Well, we know that Lady Isabella haunts this house. We have experienced first-hand her indomitable will and malice.'

He stared through the window at the gathering darkness. Night was falling but it was a silent one, no sound of that cold, biting wind. He got up and went closer to the mullioned pane.

'It's stopped snowing,' he observed. 'Though there's a fair sprinkling on the ground.'

'Oliver!' Emma exclaimed in exasperation. 'Don't start talking and then change the subject. You know that's vexatious!'

'Come with me,' Oliver said enigmatically.

Emma sighed and followed her brother into the library where he pulled the bell rope. A few minutes later Stokes appeared, hands by his side. Emma always smiled because Stokes reminded her so much of a soldier, one of those stiff subalterns she had met when she had attended regimental parties.

'Stokes, I don't want to bother Lady Alice but there are portraits all over this Hall. Do you know if there is one of a Lady Margaret Seaton? She died just after the turn of the century?'

'Of course, sir. Lady Margaret was quite a character. There's a painting on the second gallery, it's not very well done, that's why it has been put up there.'

'If you could show us?' Oliver asked.

They followed the butler up the stairs. The Hall was busy, the chambermaids taking fresh towels and sheets up to the rooms. Candles were lit and sweet smells drifted up from the kitchen. Oliver found it hard to accept that this was a house haunted by evil spirits. Nevertheless, he noticed how the maids never met his eys. Oh, they smiled, bobbed and curtseyed but, as he walked behind his sister, he caught one making the sign against the evil eye, her thumb stuck between her fingers.

The second gallery was cold.

'It always is,' Stokes muttered. 'Some of the window glass is very old. Won't it be marvellous, sir, when we have gas? They say it can turn a house into a fairy palace. Now, where has Lady Margaret gone?' He lit a candelabra standing on one of the tables and, for a while, walked up and down, a dark figure in a pool of light. Now and again he paused to study the different portraits. 'Ah yes,' he called out. 'Here we are!'

Oliver and Emma approached. The painting was in an ornate, gold-embossed frame, the colours very dark. They took one look and exclaimed in surprise.

'Is there anything the matter, sir?' Stokes asked.

Oliver stared at the long white face in the portrait, the dark dress, the hair piled up. He was certain of it.

'Stokes, is it possible?' he asked, 'for this portrait to be brought down to the library? I'd like to study it in a better light?'

'Of course, sir.'

They returned to the library, Stokes muttering at how heavy the portrait was.

'One day,' he declared, 'we'll have to do something about them. The plaster on the walls is quite old and the weight of some of these pictures . . .'

He laid it down on a table. Oliver asked for more candles to be brought then both he and Emma studied the painting.

'I can't believe it,' Emma exclaimed. 'She's garbed in nineteenth-century dress but look, Oliver, those eyes, that sneer round the mouth. You'd think they were sisters!'

'That's what I thought,' Oliver agreed. 'There's no blood tie between Margaret and Isabella. Nevertheless, this portrait reveals a similarity of spirit. And look, in the background, the painter has depicted the outline of Candleton: the gatehouse, the Tudor chimneypots. Now, in the far corner.' Oliver took his handkerchief out and wiped away some of the dust.

Emma glimpsed a circle with a triangle within it. At the centre of the triangle was an eye. Around the circle were signs of the zodiac.

'What does that mean?' she asked.

'Some people would dismiss it as mere nonsense,' Oliver replied. 'Or as a good luck symbol. Others would argue that Lady Margaret, despite living in an enlightened age, dabbled in the black arts.'

Oliver was now dusting the rest of the painting, cleaning away a thick film of dust. As he did so, Emma stared at the face of the dead woman. The more she did, the deeper her apprehension grew.

At first sight the face looked pale, not very well painted but, the more she scrutinised it, the more it seemed to come to life: those eyes, cold and implacable; the red lips ready to part in a sneer. Lady Margaret had turned her head slightly sideways, an arrogant, condescending pose. Emma sensed what her brother was about to say.

'It can't be!' she declared. 'Surely that can't happen?'

'It's possible. This Hall is haunted by a Presence. If this Presence can enter rooms, create an atmosphere, frighten and oppress, why can't it possess a human being?' He tapped the portrait with his fingers. 'Let's go back to the muniment room.'

When they entered he locked the door behind them.

'What happens?' he continued. 'If this spirit can possess another human being? Seek an entry into his or her soul?' He sat down. 'Take this Lady Thérèse from the seventeenth century. She apparently fought back but, in the end, she lost. She was declared insane and marooned on that island in the centre of the mere. Deserted by family and friends, she eventually hanged herself.

'Now we have this Lady Margaret. She comes from Northumberland. We know little about her. I suspect her son had her private papers and letters burnt. While the historians of this Hall tend to ignore her, a veritable skeleton in the family cupboard. Anyway,' Oliver spread his hands, 'Sir Maurice is a typical eighteenth-century Seaton. He divides his time between hunting and managing his estates. He is also a soldier and goes abroad with his regiment where he is killed.

'At home his young wife Margaret is left to her own devices. She is lonely, vulnerable, perhaps there's a gap in her spiritual defences. This time the Lady of the Hall does not fight back and, to quote the words of the gospel, the evil finds a home in her. Lady Margaret undergoes a metamorphosis: as the years pass, she becomes less herself and more like Isabella.'

'And this could happen again?'

'I think it already has,' Oliver replied. 'Time and again through the history of this Hall, the wives of the Seatons experienced . . .' He glanced towards the door and lowered his voice. 'Well, to put it bluntly, experienced what Lady Alice has. Now, for each person it's different. Some could have found it easy to withstand. Others never lived long enough to experience the horrors . . .' He stopped and stared down at the table.

'But others,' Emma finished the sentence for him, 'made themselves vulnerable and that might include our hostess?'

Oliver nodded. 'Sooner or later,' he murmured. 'And better sooner than later, I must have a very honest discussion with Lady Alice if I am to make progress.'

Emma walked back to the pile of documents on her table.

'What happened to Lady Margaret?' He asked.

Emma picked up a yellowing, tattered newspaper, the print slightly faded. 'Lady Margaret appears to have suffered some mysterious accident. Very few details are given out. This article describes the preparations for her funeral.' She sifted among the papers and took out a small hand-bill. 'This was published a few months later in the summer of 1805, after the English navy had defeated Napoleon's fleet at Trafalgar. The writer rejoices in the victory and claims that the tenants of Candleton will also rejoice under their new lord while Lady Margaret's death in the mere was God's judgement.'

'So,' Oliver commented. 'Either suicide or an accident?'

Suddenly there was the most terrible crash from the library. Oliver and Emma unlocked the door and ran through just as Stokes, followed by two chambermaids, rushed in at the far end.

'Heavens above!'

The butler stopped. The painting Oliver had left on the table had been picked up and flung with great force down the library. The golden frame was now shattered, the painting had slipped out. Oliver gazed around. No windows were open. He was about to pick it up when one of the chambermaids screamed, pointing at the table. An inkwell had been overturned, its dark-blue liquid snaking out. This had been used to form bold, large letters. 'Do you think I'm frightened of you, canting, snivelling priest?'

Even as Oliver stared, the ink swirled and merged, blotting out the letters.

'No one came in here?' he asked Stokes.

The butler, pale-faced, shook his head, jowls quivering, mouth half open.

'Leave us,' Emma said. 'Go back to your duties. We will see to this.'

'What's the matter?' Lady Alice came into the library accompanied by Meddlecott, his coat still wet. Emma vaguely recalled hearing a carriage arrive on the gravel path outside. Oliver waited until the butler closed the library door. He picked up the portrait and put it on the table.

'Ah, Lady Margaret, one of my more notorious predecessors,' Lady Alice said. 'Do you know, Father, I've never liked this painting.'

'And, if the evidence is to be believed,' Meddlecott added wryly, 'neither does the Presence.' Meddlecott peeled off his damp gloves. 'I've just delivered a baby in the village,' he declared. 'Everyone was happy. A bouncing baby boy; the mother is fine. And now this!'

'It's a good sign,' Oliver replied.

He took Lady Alice's hands. They were ice-cold, her gaze faltered. What is the matter? Oliver thought. Why are you so frightened? What are you hiding?

'A good sign?' Lady Alice withdrew her hand.

Oliver collected shards of the picture frame and put them on the table.

'If one of those gentlemen from London who engage in psychical research were here, they'd call this poltergeist activity.'

'Why is it a good sign?' the doctor snapped.

'I'm sorry. I don't mean to be patronising. What I'm trying to say, in a very clumsy way, is that the Presence resents what we are doing. In life she's showed her anger, why not in death?

Lady Margaret is no longer of use to her. She wants . . .'

'I'll have this removed,' Lady Alice abruptly interrupted. 'Put up in one of the attics to be repaired.' She glanced at Oliver. 'You will join us for supper?'

'When I am finished.' The priest realised he was treading on dangerous ground.

Meddlecott was about to escort Lady Alice out, but he paused in the doorway.

'When I was being brought here the driver talked about the ruins on the far side of the park, stories he had heard in the Rowan Tree, that's the tavern in Candleton High Street. Locals, even the poachers, claim the ruins are haunted. Strange lights are seen at night, the sound of men singing . . .'

'What's it like outside?' Oliver asked absentmindedly.

'Cold, the snow has stopped falling and the clouds are breaking up.'

'I'll walk down to the ruins,' Oliver said. 'I'm curious.'

'Why is that?' Lady Alice came back down the library.

'Well, the monastery was dissolved in 1535. Lady Isabella acted most ruthlessly. Now the Greyfriars community had been reformed. The monks were living a life of considerable ascetic piety. They were well-liked and respected in the area. I know this from the records. The villagers and tenants of Candleton actually petitioned Lady Isabella for the community to be saved.'

'And what was Lady Isabella's response?'

'As you might expect. Royal troops were brought from Norwich. The good brothers were shown the door. Lady Isabella pillaged the buildings, then she and the Crown shared out their ill-gotten gains. I think it's strange,' Oliver added hastily, fearful lest his companions would think he was lecturing them, 'because, if Greyfriars is haunted, I doubt if it has anything to do with Lady Isabella. Who knows?' he murmured. 'It might even be a source of strength.'

He wandered back into the muniment room. Emma raised her eyes heavenwards and followed him.

'Are you really going out there?' she asked, closing the door behind him.

'In a while. Supper won't be ready for another two hours. You continue with Lady Margaret. I am trying to break this cipher.'

They returned to their searches. Now and again Oliver would stare out of the window. He did not want to alarm Emma but he felt uncomfortable. He was being watched.

He must have sat for half an hour twiddling with his pencil, moving the letters around. Then he gave a cry of surprise, dropped the pencil and clapped his hands.

'Eureka, Emma! I've done it! I've done it!'

Emma came round the table. Oliver could barely sit still for excitement.

'Look! These words, "IND: EOE: GOC: ONF: IDO", were found on the tomb of Peter Rivers, chaplain to Lady Isabella. They are broken up into sets of three letters. They mean nothing. However, run all the letters together and you get this: "INDEOEGOCONFIDO". Now, break up the letters into words and it reads: "*In Deo ego confido*".'

Emma did so. 'The first words mean: "In God . . .".'

'Exactly,' Oliver declared, rubbing his hands. 'It's a simple phrase. "In God I trust".' He picked up the thin, calfskin-bound tome bearing the confession and opened it. 'Thank God. It's not in Latin. Now, apply the cipher and the first sentence reads: "A full and true confession",' he paused, dividing the words out in the first line, ' "of Peter Rivers, Chaplain of Candleton Manor, the Year of Our Lord 1554".'

Emma could see that the cipher used on the tomb was identical to that in the manuscript.

'But not now.' Oliver put his pencil down. 'We've sat here long enough. Let's collect our coats and hats and walk across to the ruins.'

They tidied up the muniment room, Oliver restacking the papers carefully. He put the confession and the few notes he had made back into one of the trunks and secured it carefully. Emma picked up a snuffer and extinguished the candles. She then joined her brother, unaware of the cadaverous, ghostly face pressed against the window pane.

A quarter of an hour later, dressed against the weather, they left Candleton and crossed the frozen moat, taking the winding path down to the ruins of Greyfriars monastery.

The night was bitingly cold. As the darkness closed around them, Emma concealed her disquiet. She had been associated with her brother's work for some time but Candleton was different. Now and again she'd stop and turn, lifting the lantern she carried.

'If we are being followed,' Oliver remarked, 'there is nothing we can do.'

'But it's dangerous,' Emma declared. 'If you were pushed down those stairs and that painting was hurled with such force?'

'Everything,' Oliver replied, 'is under God's guidance. We are being frightened off, Emma.' He raised his voice. 'But it will not be as easy to send us packing.'

They walked on, their boots scrunching on the gravel. A fox sped across their path. An owl, feathery wings extended, glided over them in its nightly hunt.

'Do you like Dr Meddlecott?' Oliver asked, eager to distract his sister.

'Yes, yes, I do,' Emma replied. 'He's a good, decent man. But, if and when I fall in love, Oliver, I don't want my brother to be matchmaker.' She slipped her arm through his. 'Do you remember?' she whispered. 'When we used to steal out at night to watch the foxes playing?'

'Even then you weren't afraid of the dark. Will you ever go back to our house?' he asked.

'Not for some time. I've rented it out. It's a house which

should have children. To go back alone would awake memories: bitter-sweet ones to come and haunt me.'

'But they would be friendly ones,' Oliver teased.

'It would be sad,' Emma replied. 'Every stick of furniture, every nook and cranny.' She shook her head. 'I couldn't be there alone. And you? Is this going to be your life, Oliver? Moving from house to house? Candleton is comfortable but it's not home.'

Her brother, as usual, refused to be drawn.

'We'll be there soon,' he replied.

They came to the top of a hill and, in the small valley below, made out the outlines of the ruins. They went down the path and through the small wicket gate.

'Be careful,' Oliver warned.

They both stepped gingerly. Oliver chattered about how this place would be the refectory, that would be the dormitory.

At last they found themselves in the ruins of the old nave. Only the far east wall of the church still stood in its entirety. Oliver pointed to the ruined columns on either side of this.

'Over there would be the transepts,' he said. 'And see where the ground dips in front of us, that's the steps to the sanctuary where the brothers would have their stalls.'

Emma gazed about her. Oliver had taken her to such ruins before and she could imagine the small monastery church: the rood screen which would divide the sanctuary, the dark transepts, the Galilee porch. She could even make out the outline of the huge rose window high in the east wall which would flood the sanctuary with coloured light.

For a while they just walked around. As they did so Oliver experienced a sense of peace and calm. They moved briskly, stamping their feet on the ground to keep warm.

They crossed to see some of the outbuildings, Oliver chattering so excitedly, Emma wondered if he had forgotten the real reason for their visit here.

'What are we waiting for?' she asked sharply.

Oliver just waved his hands, tapping at the loose rubble with his cane. He continued moving around the ruins but, as the manor clock began to strike six, he walked briskly back through the ruined porchway and stared down the nave.

A slight mist had rolled in. Now and again the light of the full moon was blotted out by the scurrying clouds.

'Why now?' Emma asked.

'The time of Vespers,' Oliver replied. 'People have heard singing.'

They stood and waited. Emma stared so hard, her neck began to ache. At first she thought her eyes were playing tricks upon her: sparks of light, as if candles had been lit, were moving in the misty air.

'I can see them,' Oliver murmured.

'Jack o'lanterns,' Emma said. 'Will-o-the-wisps. The land is marshy around here.'

They stood and waited. Faintly, as if from afar, came the sound of chanting. Oliver could make out the words: '*Deus in adjutorium me intende.*' The opening verse of the psalm, '*O Lord, arise and hasten to help me.*'

Sometimes the lights dimmed or the singing faded. Now and again they would flare up and the voices would sound full and strong.

Oliver walked down the church. He reached the ruined steps leading into the sanctuary. Emma followed. The closer she approached, the mist seemed to fade as did the lights and the singing. She followed her brother to where the high altar must have been.

'There's nothing here,' Emma exclaimed. 'I wonder . . .'

The subtle fragrance of incense filled the air. Emma felt warm as if fires had been lit all around her. The sweet smell of beeswax candles was also noticeable. Oliver was staring around, smiling to himself, tapping the cane on the paving stones.

'I've never seen the likes of this before,' he declared.

'Is it a haunting?' Emma asked. 'Are there such things as benevolent ghosts?'

'Possibly. This is hallowed ground. Good priests and brothers celebrated Mass and prayed here for centuries. What we have experienced could be simply a memory. Or . . .' He paused.

'Or what?'

'Well the monks were expelled forcibly and with great cruelty. Another sin Lady Isabella must answer for.'

'You mean they could be returning?'

'That may be.' Oliver tapped his cane against the floor. 'When I was in the chapel earlier in the day, a thought occurred to me. I am going to say a Mass in reparation for the great evil done at Candleton. I think I'll say it here.'

Emma shivered. The warmth and the pleasing fragrances had disappeared.

'You are not going to give up, are you?' she asked.

'No,' Oliver replied, 'I will not. If I cannot exorcise the Presence from Candleton then I will never carry out an exorcism again!'

Chapter 11

The Presence hovered around the Hall. Its consciousness was not aware of the seasons or the time of day: for it, the soil was always an iron-red, the trees black remnants of what they should have been: the sky an orangeish hue where a black sun and moon for ever hung. No sound of birds, only the cries of those in pain. Other Presences acknowledged it, not directly but through awareness and subservience to its dominance.

The Hall and the individuals who peopled it were also immaterial, except for the threats they might pose or the help and assistance they might give. The Presence could move with a speed of thought and, in an instant, bring into scrutiny anything or anyone. It moved as if across a huge painting in which time and space meant nothing. The Presence was as aware of dark images in its world as it was of the activity, the will and the intelligence of those who moved within its fiefdom, what it considered to be its own, Candleton Hall.

The woman, Lady Alice, was vulnerable, made more so by herself; the physician, the Presence scorned as able to offer physical comfort but nothing else. The priest was proving different: his presence was most offensive and threatening. He might change this world, call on those who awaited beyond the garish horizon and that sliver of brilliant light which divided earth and sky.

The Presence moved from the Hall into the ruins now vacated by the priest and his woman. A place of desolation – the Presence could sense its bleakness – of desires roughly frustrated, work cruelly interrupted; souls displaced, harmony shattered. No longer blessed but made profane by terrible sacrilege.

The Presence very rarely haunted these ruins, which provoked memories, feelings of disquiet. However, it was now alarmed and its malicious glee was turning sour. Its will was being challenged by other sounds and feelings hostile to it, foreign to its world. A chanting had begun, soft and faint, which interfered with its concentration of thought and the full intent of its will.

The Presence had experienced such feelings before but this was different. The chanting brought back an awareness of another world: of sins committed, wrongs done and the demand for reparation. Stranger still, columns of light, thin pillars of burning fire, now glowed on the edge of its consciousness. These seemed to be connected with the chanting of men whose world had been destroyed. Could that be possible? Even in wondering the Presence experienced a vulnerability and weakness. It moved swiftly like a person blinking in a sharp burst of sunlight. The Presence wanted to remove these doubts, these anxieties from its vision. Yet, like the sunlight they remained: a faint stream of disquietude.

The murderous anger at the heart of this sinister being boiled and bubbled like water in a cauldron ready to spill over. The Presence, using the power it had invoked, lashed out against the eastern wall of the church, crumbling the moss-covered stones. If it could only destroy, wipe out what this place represented!

Oliver sat in the muniment room, pencil to his lips. He studied the confession of Father Peter: the opening sentences spilling out so clearly, so sharply Oliver felt he was in a confessional and hearing, down the years, the anxieties and fears of this venerable old man.

Oliver had joined the rest for supper, a rather quiet affair. Lady Alice had picked at her food. Emma had been distracted by Dr Meddlecott while Oliver had been impatient to return to his studies. Now and again there was forced gaiety. Dr Meddlecott would tell a funny story, Lady Alice would laugh, but this was to hide her fear and deepening apprehension.

Afterwards Lady Alice had gone up to bed, Emma and the doctor retiring to the small drawing room where the physician had promised that he would show her how to cheat at cards.

Oliver put his pencil down. The house was quiet. Stokes had come in and lit all the available candles. The door to the library stood ajar. The butler had returned offering Oliver a cup of chocolate and a glass of brandy. The priest had scarcely touched these and the chocolate had grown cold. Oliver turned back to the beginning of his transcript.

In the name of God the Father, Son and Holy Ghost, Amen. I, Peter Rivers, chaplain of Candleton, do hereby confess that which has been told me. I cannot break the seal of the confessional but I am old and sickly. Before I die I need to tell of the hideous things which have been entrusted to me by Mathilda, daughter of Sir Henry Seaton. I do so in this secret cipher not to confuse but, if God wills it, these things can be revealed in a time and a place of His own good choosing . . .

Oliver raised his head. He could hear footsteps outside on the gravelled path, running backwards and forwards like a child at play. He glanced down at his writing. The letters seemed to liquefy, to swim on the page. Oliver blinked and looked up. The footsteps crunched the gravel outside as the small casement window was abruptly flung open. The cold night breeze rushed in, dousing the candles in one quick rush of air. Oliver crossed himself and got to his feet. He went to the window.

'Oliver! Oliver! I'm here! Can you find me?'

Arthur's voice, so clear, so precise, full of laughter as it always was.

'Oliver, where are you? Come and find me! I've been waiting so long!'

Again the footsteps.

'Oliver!'

The tone was now strident, rather hurtful. The priest slammed the window shut. He wasn't frightened but angry.

'How dare she?' he whispered. 'How dare she play tricks with memories so sweet and sacred?'

Oliver relit the candles. Though he felt sleepy but he was determined to finish this translation and he sat down, closing his ears to the plaintive cries from outside.

In her great four-poster bed Lady Alice was aware of being asleep. Images came and went. She moved restlessly, half aware that, if she woke, perhaps she would finish the brandy Ruth had brought up; anything to make her forget. Lady Alice rolled on her back, opened her eyes and stared into the darkness.

'Why?' she muttered.

She was about to roll back but stiffened. Someone else was lying next to her. Lady Alice felt panic see the within her. She recalled Father Oliver's warning that such phenomena might occur! She must control her fear, not give way to it.

She lay rigid, not daring to move or stretch out her hand. Prayers from her childhood echoed through her brain but the words were confused and jumbled.

'Our Father Who art in Heaven. Angel of God, my guardian dear . . .'

Lady Alice broke free from her freezing panic. The night light on the table at the end of the bed had gone out. Pulling herself gently up, Lady Alice eased herself out of the bed. For a while her fingers fumbled but at last she found a tinder and struck a light. She really wanted to run for the door, go out into the gallery and scream for help but how long could she keep doing that?

She turned slowly, the pool of light following her. On the

bolsters lay her dead husband: he, who should be buried in the cold clay of the graveyard. His face looked as it was in life, the vein-streaked nose, the weather-beaten cheeks, those glassy blue eyes staring implacably at her as they would when he was angry. Lady Alice felt her throat constrict, her stomach clench in spasms. She stretched her hand out, but the icy-blue eyes did not blink. The flesh was cold.

Lady Alice ran for the door, coughing and retching. She hurtled out into the gallery. In the darkness behind her came a shuffling movement as if whatever was there stirred to follow her. Blindly she ran along the gallery, the hot wax dripping onto her fingers. She blew the candle out and let it fall, crashing and bouncing to the floor. Lady Alice reached Emma's room. Pulling back the bed drapes, she shook the sleeping figure.

'Wake up! Wake up for Heaven's sake!'

The figure turned, the sheets falling back. Lady Alice screamed. It was not Emma Grafeld but the woman in the portrait, the eyes full of malicious glee. Lady Alice crumpled to the floor. Screaming dinned her ears but it wasn't coming from her. She couldn't scream! She would just lie there and let these terrors of the night take her.

In the muniment room, Oliver heard the terrible screams followed by the sound of running footsteps. He went out into the main hallway. Dr Meddlecott and Emma were already hurrying up the stairs and along the gallery above, doors were opening and shutting to the shouts of servants. He went up.

At the door to Emma's bedchamber, Stokes was gently shoo-ing the servants away. He allowed Oliver through. Lady Alice was seated on the floor, her back to the bed, hands fluttering in front of her face as if she was trying to join them in prayer.

'Fetch my bag!' Meddlecott snapped. 'You'll find it just within the doorway.'

Stokes hurried off. Oliver closed the bedroom door and helped Emma and the doctor to lift Lady Alice. They tried to place her on the bed but she fought back, clawing the air with her hands. At last they made her comfortable in a chair. Emma took her hands, stroking them gently, pushing back the hair from her face. Dr Meddlecott seized Lady Alice's wrist, feeling for the pulse.

'She's in shock,' he declared. 'God knows what happened up here?'

'She must have seen something.' Emma stroked Lady Alice's hair. 'You saw something, didn't you? And you came to me for help? But I wasn't here.'

Lady Alice, eyes vacant, nodded.

'But we are here now,' Emma added soothingly. 'Nothing will happen.'

Stokes returned with Meddlecott's heavy valise of medicines. The doctor coaxed Lady Alice to take the opiate, forcing the small glass between her lips, pressing back her head so she would swallow it. Oliver sat on the large trunk at the foot of the bed and watched. Now and again Lady Alice would look at him but then avert her gaze. They must have sat with her for half an hour. Gradually she calmed down as exhaustion and the effects of the opiate made itself felt.

Ruth came in. She and Emma took the now-drowsy Lady Alice back to her bedchamber. Ruth, pale-faced and trying to calm her own fears, begged Emma to stay with her mistress. She agreed. A relieved Stokes immediately ordered servants to find the most comfortable cot bed and have it placed in their mistress's chamber.

Once they were gone, Meddlecott busied himself tidying things away in his bag. From the hallway below the clock chimed midnight.

'Ah well,' he sighed. 'I'll be sleeping here tonight.'

'But that's not on your mind, is it, Doctor?'

'No, no it isn't.' Meddlecott loosened his broad cravat and undid the high starched collar beneath.

'Let me guess.' Oliver sat down on a chair. 'You are going to tell me that my arrival here has made matters worse not better?'

'I am glad you said it, Father. You put it more tactfully than I would have done.'

'I did not wish to come here. I was sent by Archbishop Manning at Lady Alice's request.'

'Lady Alice is ill,' Meddlecott snapped. 'She is sick in mind and body. I do not think your presence is helping. I am sorry,' he added, 'but Lady Alice is my patient.'

'And so what do you propose?'

'Lady Alice should leave Candleton for a while. It will do her good. She has a cottage on the other side of the village, it's well equipped.'

'By all means,' Oliver agreed. 'But I don't think that will do any good.' Oliver went to open the door, to ensure no one was listening outside. 'You've got to believe me. This is not Lady Alice being hysterical or the phantasms of a tired or fevered brain. Hauntings like this do not happen unless there is a purpose.'

'What do you mean?'

'Lady Alice is that purpose. Try as you might, and I am more than prepared to help, but I don't think Lady Alice will be allowed to leave Candleton.'

Meddlecott picked up his brandy glass and sipped from it. He stared down, scuffing the carpet with the toe of his boot.

'I'd like to take her away but you think she'll be stopped?'

'You are a doctor, Meddlecott: you heal the mind and body. You have text books which list this or that illness, you divide them into physical and mental but you, I, Lady Alice, we are more than that. We are immortal souls, an area of experience which cannot come under scientific scrutiny. It's the world of the metaphysical.' Oliver paused. 'If this haunting continues it will be very serious for Lady Alice because it's her soul which will end up being haunted.'

'You mean possessed?'

'Yes, what the Church calls possession. It's happened before in the history of Candleton and it could happen again. You are her ladyship's physician, I think the time has come for bluntness and honesty. I believe Lady Alice has not been fully truthful with me. No, no,' Oliver shook his head at Meddlecott's grimace of distaste, 'she is hiding something in her soul, which is affecting her mind, her body, it could even affect her unborn child.'

'But you have . . .?'

'Oh, don't talk of proof or evidence. I'm not a policeman, I'm here to help.'

Meddlecott put the brandy glass down and drummed his fingers on the table.

'I'm going to tell you what I know.' He glanced at Oliver. 'I'm speaking as a physician to a Catholic priest. I have you oath, as a man and a priest, that you will keep this matter confidential?'

Oliver held up his right hand. 'You have my oath.'

'I believe,' Meddlecott began, 'that when Lady Alice married Sir Thomas, she really loved him and he her. Oh, Sir Thomas wasn't a bad man. He was fond of his hunting, his horses and his dogs. He wasn't romantic; I doubt if he had the imagination to be so but there was also a streak of nastiness in him, especially when he was drunk. He'd regret it, be fulsome in his apologies but, well it was what you'd call a spiritual weakness.

'Now, as the years passed, Lady Alice failed to give birth to a living male heir. Sir Thomas saw this as a personal insult to himself. When he was sober he was a kind, proper gentleman but, after he had been drinking, he would either sulk or become violent. In the last few months before his death, this violence got the better of him. On more than one occasion I was called to tend Lady Alice after Sir Thomas had beaten her with a riding crop. On another occasion her back was scored with savage purple weals.' He caught the surprise in Oliver's eyes. 'Lady Alice never complained. It was Sir Thomas who sent for me. He was apologetic, promised it wouldn't happen again but, unfortunately, it did.'

'And Lady Alice?'

'She bore it patiently enough, ever ready to excuse her husband but . . .'

Oliver waited.

'God forgive me!' Meddlecott murmured. 'But there were times, Father, just for a few seconds, a glance, a cast of the lips. I think there were occasions when Lady Alice really hated her husband.' He sighed. 'Not so much for the physical beating but the degradation, the humiliation.'

'And the accident?' Oliver asked.

'Ah yes, I am not too sure what happened. Lady Alice gave her husband the stirrup cup before the hunt began. I was called after the fall occurred: Sir Thomas's neck had snapped like a twig.'

'Did you carry out a full autopsy?'

Meddlecott shuffled his feet. 'I did but, there again, I didn't.' He took his fob watch out and looked at it. 'I'll be honest, I was too frightened. Sir Thomas was a superb horseman, one of the best in his brigade. The hedge was high but the horse was an experienced hunter. Nevertheless, from what I saw, I judged it to be an accident.'

'But you did wonder?'

'Yes, Father, I wondered. What happens if Sir Thomas was given a drink which made him unsteady, some potion to unseat his balance, to make him less prudent? The corpse stayed above ground for five days before burial. I inspected it on more than one occasion. I saw nothing which provoked my suspicions. Nevertheless, I made enquiries. Lady Alice does not travel. She rarely goes to London while . . .'

'Candleton does not have a pharmacy?' Oliver completed his sentence.

'Yes, Father, Candleton village does not have a pharmacy. Moreover, since Sir Thomas's death, I have virtually had the run of this house. If Lady Alice had bribed one of her maids or servants to bring her such a potion they would have chattered.' He sighed, blowing out his cheeks. 'Indeed, the more I searched, the more I believe Lady Alice was totally innocent.'

'Why are you so sure? I know,' Oliver added hastily, 'like you, I believe Lady Alice is a true Christian woman.'

'As I said,' Meddlecott continued, 'Sir Thomas loved his drink. I did not attend the banquet held here for other members of the Hunt the night before he died but, from what I gather, Sir Thomas had to be carried up to his chambers.'

'So, he could have still been drunk when he mounted his horse the following morning?'

'Possibly. And the stirrup cup wouldn't have helped.'

'What does Lady Alice think?'

'Ah! As Shakespeare says, Father.' He smiled. 'I know from your sister you are a devotee of the playwright. "There's the rub". Lady Alice may be totally innocent but I do wonder if she thinks that she might be guilty? Ever since I met her, long before Sir Thomas's death, and don't take offence Father, but Lady Alice betrayed all the symptoms of guilt you associate with a Catholic. Guilt about not being a good mother; guilt about not being a good wife; guilt that she did not do more for the Seaton family, the estates. Oh,' he waved a hand, 'the list is endless. More importantly, she always confessed to a sense of unease at Candleton, of being watched. Sir Thomas used to laugh at her: he said that Lady Alice was getting more like his mother every day.'

'I beg your pardon?'

'Lady Charlotte,' Meddlecott replied. 'Sir Thomas's mother. Apparently she also complained of being scrutinised, of a sense of disquiet.' Meddlecott shrugged. 'However, from what I gather, nothing happened. Lady Charlotte died rather young.'

Oliver rose to his feet, tired and weary.

'You still intend to take Lady Alice away?'

'I do, Father.'

'And there's nothing I can do to persuade you against it?'

'Father, I am her physician. I must do what I think is best for my patient.'

Oliver had no choice but to agree. He bade Meddlecott goodnight and returned to his own chamber. He meant to prepare properly for bed but he lay down fully clothed and, before he realised, drifted into a deep sleep.

He was woken early just before dawn by a loud rapping on the door and Meddlecott's insistent call. Oliver staggered to his feet. He dashed some cold water over his face. Meddlecott and Lady Alice were waiting in the hallway below.

'Good morning, Father.' Lady Alice's face was pale with shadows under her eyes. She looked a little unsteady on her feet, Meddlecott held her gently under her arm.

'I'm sorry about last night,' she apologised. 'I had dreadful dreams. I would much prefer to stay . . .'

'I think it's best,' Meddlecott broke in. 'The carriage is ready. Father Oliver and I will take you only a short distance, to one of the cottages on the other side of Candleton.'

'Can Ruth come with me?'

'In a little while,' Meddlecott replied. 'But it's best if you left as quietly and as quickly as possible. If we arouse the household it will only cause suspicion and alarm. Father Oliver will come with you.'

Stokes brought Oliver's coat, hat and cane. The priest felt tempted to argue with Meddlecott's decisions but the physician looked so determined Oliver decided to let matters take their course.

The coach, a Clarence, was waiting in the courtyard.

Thompson was up on the driver's seat, muffled against the biting wind. The horses, two docile bays, were fully harnessed. While Meddlecott helped Lady Alice into the carriage Oliver swung himself up onto the seat beside Thompson.

'You should stay inside, Father. It's too bloody cold up here. God knows why I have to do this. Ah well, at least it's not snowing and the journey's not far.'

Meddlecott had got out of the coach and was looking up at him. 'Father Oliver, join us inside.'

'I prefer to stay here,' the priest replied. 'I can be of more help.'

'Well, if you change your mind.' Meddlecott climbed back into the coach.

There was a rap on the roof, Thompson cracked his whip, turning the horses out through the gateway.

'Drive slowly,' Oliver whispered.

'Father, you do my job and I'll do mine. I've driven horses since I was knee high to a buttercup. Her Ladyship's safe with me and . . .'

'It's not a question of that.' Oliver tried not to snap. 'I am just a little frightened about what might happen. Please: if you reach the end of the drive and nothing has happened, then dismiss me as a fanciful fool.'

Behind his muffler, Thompson's eyes crinkled in amusement.

'All right, Father, have it your own way.' He shook the reins. 'Come on girls!'

The carriage bowled through the gatehouse and across the moat.

'A hard morning,' Thompson muttered.

Oliver agreed. The sky was cloud-free but an iron hoarfrost had turned the parkland into a shimmering sea of ice. The horses' hooves skittered on the gravelled path, the carriage swayed slightly. Oliver had to bend his head to avoid the cold wind and he held on to the brim of his hat.

Thompson was true to his word. He kept the horses steady, the carriage rolling smoothly until, abruptly, the horses stopped just beyond the moat. Trained cobs, they showed no excitement but faltered and, despite Thompson flapping the reins quietly and urging them on, both horses stood stock-still.

'What in Heaven's name has got into them?' Thompson climbed off his seat and went to the carriage window.

Meddlecott pulled up the flap.

'Is anything wrong?'

'I don't know, sir. Never seen the likes of it before! Still as statues they are.'

Oliver climbed down. He walked along and gently stroked the muzzle of one of the horses, staring into the half-light.

'What's wrong, girl?' he murmured. 'What do you see?'

The horse snorted and shook its head. Thompson came round and tried to urge them forward. The horses stubbornly refused to move.

'Something's frightened them.'

'Perhaps a rabbit or a fox?' Thompson was now losing his temper. 'Come on girls! Don't be bloody stupid!'

The horses became restive. One of them shook its head and, if it hadn't been for the traces, would have reared up.

'All right! All right!' Thompson said soothingly. 'Hey! Whoa!'

Both horses now began to move backwards, a clumsy jostling movement. Meddlecott sprang from the carriage and, while Thompson quietened the horses, helped Lady Alice out. Oliver now walked ahead, tapping his cane, searching the ground. Perhaps Thompson was right: horses refused to go forward if there was a dead animal in their path but, in this faint light, he could see nothing untoward. Oliver was about to tell Thompson this when something caught his eye.

At first he thought someone was walking up the lane towards them, shadowy outline. His mouth went dry and the nape of his neck prickled with cold fear. The shape was not on the path but hovering just above it. Oliver could make out no features, nothing, just a shadow moving backwards and forwards, like black smoke from a roaring fire. Oliver took a step forwards and crossed himself.

'Who are you?' he whispered.

The shape moved, hurtling towards him. Oliver closed his eyes and flinched at a rush of icy, stinking air, the smell of a charnel house, of rottenness which brought back memories of the slums in Seven Dials. He staggered, missed his footing and fell. Behind him Thompson was shouting, the carriage creaked as it was forced backwards.

Oliver scrambled to his feet. Thompson now had the horses quiet, holding them both by their harness, talking soothingly. Meddlecott, however, had already taken Lady Alice by the arm and was leading her back towards the gatehouse.

Oliver returned. Thompson, hat off, his muffler slipped and red face glistening with sweat, stared at him fearfully.

'I saw that,' he murmured. 'In God's name, Father!'

Oliver patted him on the shoulder. 'Take the carriage back,' he said quietly. 'Tell no one what you saw.'

Chapter 12

Father Oliver Grafeld stood in the ruins of Greyfriars Priory. He noticed the newly fallen masonry from the east wall and wondered if that had anything to do with the Presence. After all, the wind had been brisk but not strong enough to cause such damage though the severe cold could possibly make the masonry crack.

Oliver checked the table which Stokes and another servant had brought out to serve as an altar. It was covered with a white linen cloth with a candle horn at each end. The flame inside glowed strongly through the protective bull's-eye glass. In the centre of the altar stood a small metal crucifix, beneath which Oliver had placed a small reliquary containing a shard of the true cross. His chalice and paten were still in their case: and the vestments, black with gold trimming, which Lady Alice had loaned him, still hung over the chair Stokes had also brought.

'Why do you want to say Mass out there?' Emma had asked when they all gathered for breakfast.

'I believe I should,' Oliver replied.

He had glanced at Lady Alice, who had quickly recovered from her aborted attempt to leave Candleton. She had dressed her hair and changed from her travelling clothes to a cream silk blouse, gathered high at the neck, and a long black skirt with a taped band round the middle which allowed her, so she explained, discreetly patting her stomach, room for 'the other' she carried.

'Take the vestments from the chapel!' Lady Alice insisted. She had leant over and squeezed Oliver's hand. Her grip was firm and warm. 'Don't worry. I'm very pleased to

169

return to Candleton. I would only have become agitated as Emma is now, about you celebrating a Mass in the ruins.'

'I want to say it there for the dead; for all those who've died at Candleton over the years. As well as ask Christ to give us His special protection.'

'Is that wise?' Emma had asked tartly. She was still slightly annoyed at being excluded from Meddlecott's plan to remove Lady Alice. 'I mean, you might make yourself vulnerable.'

'I don't think so, I'll be safe.'

'Can't we be there?' Emma had asked.

'I'd prefer it if you weren't. I think it's best.' If anything untoward happens, one Grafeld should be protected.'

Within the hour everything had been set up. Stokes and the others had left; the ruins were deserted. Only a crow cawed from one of the niches high in the ruined walls.

Oliver went to the edge of the ruins. A morning mist now swirled cutting off any view of the manor, emphasising Oliver's isolation. He crossed himself.

'I must not let my imagination play tricks,' he murmured.

He began to vest: the alb, the amice, chasuble, the stole. He checked the offertory cruets, containing the water and wine, took out his chalice and paten and put them on the altar. He then genuflected on the cushion provided, stood up and began his lonely Mass.

'*In Nomine Patris, et Filii* . . . I will go unto the altar of God, to God who gave joy to my youth.'

Oliver's voice echoed round the ruins. Usually he had an altar boy to make the replies. Now he stopped and whispered the responses himself.

He approached the altar and paused. When Greyfriars had been a thriving monastery, this was where the high altar must have stood, the crowning glory of their church, dominating the sanctuary. Oliver experienced a sharp feeling of desolation at such physical and spiritual beauty being destroyed so quickly yet so permanently. He wondered if this was the first Mass celebrated here since the monastery's dissolution. He sighed, opened his breviary at the Mass of the Dead and read the Collect, then the Epistle, a reading from one of the letters from St Paul.

By the time he reached the Gospel, Oliver felt more comfortable though increasingly aware of other sensations. He was no longer cold. The sharp morning breeze had disappeared and, now and again, he smelt the faint fragrance of incense as well as that of hundreds of beeswax candles.

He proceeded to the Offertory, pouring the wine into the chalice, saying the prayers from memory, then the Lavabo where the priest symbolically washed his fingers in preparation for the sacred rite.

'*Lavabo manus inter innocentes* . . . I will wash my hands amongst the innocent, Oh Lord,' he murmured.

'And encompass Thine altar . . .'

'*Ut audeam vocem* . . . that I may hear the voice of Your praise and tell of all Your marvellous works.'

Oliver stopped. The response had been a whisper as if someone was standing beside him joining in this priestly prayer. He continued and the whisper grew as if a group of other priests were following him in this psalm of praise.

When he had finished Oliver looked around. There was no one, but he had definitely heard the voices. Was it his imagination, voices within his own mind? Or had those priests who celebrated Mass here so long ago come back to join him? Oliver continued slowly; there was silence until he reached the point just before the great prayer of the Consecration. He spread his hands.

'The Lord be with you.'

Before he could utter the response, it was given for him.

'And with your spirit too.'

'Lift up your hearts.'

'We have lifted them up to the Lord.'

'It is right to give thanks to God.'

'It is truly right to give Him thanks and praise!'

The voices seemed to come from either side where the monks used to stand in their stalls.

Oliver continued, this time in silence, but, when he lifted his voice to say the Sanctus, 'Holy, Holy, Holy Lord God of Hosts', the voices joined in. Oliver felt tears start to his eyes, a lump to his throat. He was sure that, as the hymn of praise was delivered, he caught another voice, high, lilting and boyish: memories of Arthur flooded back.

The Mass proceeded. After the Consecration, when he reached the point where he had to pray for the dead, Oliver closed his eyes and broke from the rite.

'Give peace and life, Lord,' he urged. 'To all those who once lived, worked and died here: those who praised Your holy name. Protect us here and now.'

Oliver then swiftly proceeded with the rest of the Mass.

When it was all over, he sat in the chair, eyes closed, making his own thanksgiving. Afterwards he took his vestments off, put his cloak and hat back on, cleaned the chalice and sacred vessels and put them back in their case. Stokes had assured him of their safe return to Candleton. Oliver surveyed the ruins. He wasn't sure what had happened, but he felt comforted and strengthened.

He walked out back along the path towards the Hall. The mist had grown thicker, swirling like a stream, deadening all sound. He passed the chapel and looked to his left. The mist had shifted; he glimpsed the glinting water of the mere.

'Why not?' he said to himself. 'I've been everywhere but the island.'

He left the path and, swinging his cane, walked across the grass. Lady Alice had mentioned there was a narrow skiff or barge. Oliver had spent some time in Oxford and knew how to punt. He heard a sound and turned. At the top of the hill, among the line of trees, a rider had appeared: the horse was grey, its harness ornate. Oliver took a step forward. The figure astride it was dressed completely in white, like a shroud cloaking a corpse, a veil covering the face. Oliver experienced a terrible malevolence and recalled the line from the Book of the Apocalypse: 'And I looked, and behold a pale horse: and his name that sat on him was Death, and Hell followed after.'

The mist swirled in again. Oliver remained rooted to the spot. When the mist broke, horse and rider had disappeared.

Oliver crossed himself and continued. He found the small skiff moored to a narrow wooden jetty which ran out into the mere. He recalled the phantasm as he stared across the black, placid water, the mist shifting above it. Was it safe? He took a deep breath.

'I won't be frightened,' he whispered hoarsely. 'I won't be bullied.'

He threw his cane into the skiff and gingerly climbed in. He picked up the pole and loosened the rope, the barge moving away of its own accord. Oliver, deftly using the pole, turned its nose towards the island.

The mere was as silent as the grave. Only the water lapping against the skiff and his own grunts as he pushed at the pole broke the eerie atmosphere. He was soon across, the skiff running aground on the pebble-dotted beach. Oliver climbed out and pulled the skiff further up then, taking his cane, walked on.

At first he thought there was no paths through: the undergrowth and bushes stretched like a wall but, at last, he found a small trackway and followed it in, knocking with his cane at the brambles and weeds which now choked the path. The island seemed covered by this thick copse of trees beneath which bushes and wild vegetation rendered it desolate and eerie.

Oliver kept to the pathway which eventually led into a

clearing, a small dip in the land. The ruins in the centre were the tumbledown walls of what must have been a cottage with a small outhouse beyond. These were almost covered in gorse and prickling bramble, though parts of the wicket fencing which had once surrounded it still stood.

Oliver walked into what remained of the garden and up through the ruined doorway. A melancholy place. The cottage must have had two or three ground-floor rooms with bed-chambers above. A blackened fireplace stood against the far wall; some rotting pieces of wood, the remains of furniture, were strewn about. Birds had nested there and, by the stench, some wild animal had also turned it into its lair.

Oliver kicked at the debris on the floor and glimpsed the etching on the stone. He cleared the moss away and the tombstone became more visible. The carved writing was now filled with lichen but Oliver made out the words, 'Lady Thérèse Seaton', the date of her death and a quotation from the Bible beneath.

Oliver closed his eyes and recited the psalm for the dead. 'Out of the depths have I cried out to Thee, Oh Lord, hear my voice . . .'

This was a fearful place, still reeking of the loneliness and sadness of the poor woman who had been forced to live here as a hermit. Nevertheless, Oliver could sense nothing else, no male-volence: none of the formidable oppressive atmosphere he had experienced in the Hall. He tapped the tombstone with his cane.

'I hope you are at peace,' he said and made his way back out through the copse and down to the barge.

He deftly poled the barge back. The mist hung like a thick grey curtain. Oliver paused, peering forward, trying to catch any sound, but there was nothing except that freezing mist closing round him like a shroud.

'God help me!' Oliver prayed.

He had visions of himself going round in circles or crossing the mere to a place where he would find it difficult to disembark. He felt a wetness against his shin and stared in horror at the water which now lapped about his feet. He crouched down, feeling about in the cold, slimy water. The skiff had shown no problems on its journey across. He could find no gap or rent. Perhaps the caulking between the timbers had grown loose? Oliver stood up. If he wasn't careful the skiff would become water-logged and he would be left floundering in this icy, mist-covered mere.

'God help me!' he said again.

He was frightened, fearful that this was no ordinary accident, and recalled the malevolence of that rider.

Oliver tried to control his panic. Misty tendrils came out like the arms of a ghost to embrace him. He was a good swimmer but how long would he survive if the skiff sank? Oliver turned the skiff carefully towards where he thought the bank was.

'Oliver! Oliver!'

He breathed a sigh of relief. Emma was calling him! He glimpsed the powerful lantern she must be holding. Oliver headed straight for the light. The water was now round his ankles, cold and biting, then the nose of the skiff crunched into the bank. Oliver dropped the pole, picked up his cane and leapt on to the frosted grass. He climbed up.

'Emma!'

Now there was no light. The mist shifted. No one was standing there.

'Emma, where are you?'

The only answer was the caw of a rook. Oliver walked forward, his feet soaking. He felt a chill of apprehension and then relaxed. If he hadn't seen the lantern, if he hadn't heard that voice? He recalled the responses to his Mass at the ruins.

'*Deo gratias*,' he said quietly. 'Thank God for my deliverance!'

He walked over the parkland, across the bridge and into the

courtyard. Emma and Dr Meddlecott were just coming out, cloaked and hatted.

'We wondered where you were!' Emma exclaimed. 'Stokes went down to the ruins but could see no sign of you.' She gazed at her brother's feet.

'It's all right,' he reassured her. 'I went across to the island. Well, I got my feet wet.'

'Come in! Come in!' Emma almost pushed him across the yard.

The doctor took his hat and cane. Emma dragged her brother upstairs and stood over him while he took off his socks and shoes, then handed him a thick woollen pair of socks.

'Dry your feet and put these on, then your slippers.' She put his shoes near the fire. 'And you'd best have something to eat and drink. You must be starving!'

Oliver let her fuss him. Stokes brought up a tray of tea, hot toasted scones, some bacon and grilled muffins.

'You'd best eat here, sir. It's warmer than the small dining room.'

Oliver blessed himself and ate quickly. He recalled the misty, cold mere. That he had become lost and the skiff had broached water had been no accident. Yet, there again, Emma's voice and that lantern?

'Are you going back to your studies?'

Emma was in the doorway.

'As soon as I have finished, if you could have the candles lit and the fire built up.' Oliver put his cup down. 'Oh, Emma, have you been out of the Hall this morning?'

'No, I told you, we became concerned and were about to leave . . .'

Oliver nodded. Emma could see he was lost in one of his reveries so she closed the door.

A quarter of an hour later Oliver, looking as if he had thawed out, joined her in the muniment room.

'This is nearly over,' he declared and tapped the confession. 'I've got this ready. It's just a matter of making sense. You can either stay with me or . . .' he grinned. 'You can always go walking with Dr Meddlecott!'

He ducked as Emma scrunched up a scrap of paper and threw it at his head.

Oliver opened the confession. He read the introduction again: the chaplain, Peter Rivers, calling on God to witness that he spoke the truth. Within a few seconds of beginning to read, Oliver became lost in the anguished soul of this priest who had lived over three hundred years ago.

Emma watched her brother, pencil poised, pore over the transcript. Now and again he'd sigh and make some amendments. She sat and waited until he'd finished.

'God have mercy!' he breathed. 'May the Lord and His angels comfort this poor soul!'

'What is it?' Emma asked.

Oliver picked up the transcript. 'It's clumsy and certainly not the best translation but it's poignant, the confession of a tired, very old priest. Peter Rivers witnessed a great deal of change – dynastic wars, the Reformation, not to mention the violent chain of events at Candleton. He was an innocent man, a good priest, perhaps a little simple-witted. He was totally unaware of what was going on around him.'

'I know someone like him,' Emma teased.

Oliver smiled. 'God forgive I should be like this.' He tapped the paper with his pencil. 'You can read it but . . .' His voice trailed off.

'Tell me.'

'Rivers came here as a priest around the same time Sir Henry married Lady Isabella. He was chaplain to the Hall and to the manor community, that included the tenants and the villagers. He was innocent and naïve. He said his Mass every day, recited the divine office, visited the sick, buried the dead, baptised the children. He wasn't a brave man.' Oliver pulled a face. 'Yes, a bit like myself. When the Reformation came, he took the Oath of Supremacy and accepted Henry VIII as Head of the Church but secretly he remained a Catholic.'

'That would have been dangerous?'

'For a bishop, for a lord or a priest in a busy London parish, yes, but a rural priest?'

'And he'd be protected by Lady Isabella?'

'I doubt very much,' Oliver replied, 'if Lady Isabella cared about Heaven or Hell, let alone the finer points of Catholic theology. Nevertheless, she was cunning enough to use it as a threat over poor Rivers. He doesn't say as much but, at the beginning of the confession, he does concede that Lady Isabella was a powerful patron, a good benefactor who shielded him, in his own phrase, "against a sea of troubles".'

'So he was her man, body and soul?'

'Yes, yes, he was. However, according to his confession, Rivers really didn't believe anything was wrong at Candleton. He mentions in passing how the deaths of Sir Henry and his two sons, not to mention Lord Montague, were all seen as part of Divine Providence. In the first part of the confession,' Oliver picked up the sheaf of papers, 'Lady Isabella is much pitied. A woman of sorrows: that's the role she must have played.'

'When was it written?'

'Ah!' Oliver got up and stretched, stamping his feet. his toes still felt a little numb after the mishap on the mere. 'In poor old Chaplain Peter's eyes, all was above suspicion, until he was summoned, in the spring of 1555, to hear Mathilda's confession.'

'Sir Henry's daughter, supposedly weak in her wits, who stitched the tapestry?'

'The same one. Now, by then Lady Mathilda herself was an old woman. She had seen them all die or disappear: her father, her two brothers, Lord Montague.'

'And she wanted to tell the priest about her suspicions?'

'Well, yes. Rivers found it impossible to accept that Lady Isabella had been a murderess, a liar and an adulteress.'

'Had been?'

'Don't forget this confession was written a year after Lady Isabella disappeared. Rivers mentions all this in his preamble.

'Now, in the spring of 1555, Lady Mathilda had caught a cold, rheums in her head which slipped on to her chest, bronchitis or pneumonia. Apparently the physicians despaired of her life. Candleton was awaiting its new lord, another Seaton from London. Lady Mathilda was an old woman. The servants ignored her except for one old retainer. Mathilda, being of the Catholic faith, asked for Rivers to come and listen to her confession. Rivers did. It must have been a shocking revelation. Everything he believed in, the world in which he lived, collapsed about his ears.'

'Mathilda told him everything?'

'Oh yes. How Lady Isabella and Lord Montague had arranged the deaths of Sir Henry and one of his sons. How the other son had fled from Bosworth, returning secretly to Candleton only to be killed and his body disposed of in the woods or some other secret place.'

'How did Mathilda know this?'

'Well, it's not very clear from the confession whether Mathilda actually saw him or found something belonging to him. Anyway, she apparently produced this for Rivers. He, of course, rejected what she said, dismissing it as the wanderings of a poor, witless, old woman.'

'Yet there was more to come?'

'Of course. Mathilda, because she was considered wandering in her wits, was often ignored, told to go and be busy about her needlework. She was, in fact, busy listening at key-holes, eavesdropping on conversations. A few years after Isabella and Lord Montague were married, Mathilda confessed that she overheard a conversation between this precious pair. Lord Montague had actually warned Isabella "that he would not go the same way as her first husband".' Oliver paused. 'A few weeks later,' he continued, 'according to Mathilda, he suffered his riding accident. She claims that he was poisoned, his fall from the horse was the result of a poisoned stirrup cup handed to him by Lady Isabella.'

'Did Rivers accept this?'

'No, he argued volubly against it. Mathilda insisted, reminding the priest of how Lady Isabella had had the corpse brought back to the Hall, dressed for burial, put in a casket and buried before any trace of poison could reveal itself or the curious make observations.' Oliver walked over to the fire and, crouching down, warmed his cold, numbed fingers. 'If Rivers believed this was bad enough, worse was to follow. Mathilda told him about the tapestry: how she had woven all this into the scenes depicted there. She made Rivers take a great oath that he would personally ensure the tapestry was not destroyed or stolen. Rivers agreed.'

'And the worst was to follow?'

'Well, so far Mathilda had confessed to the sins of Lady Isabella and Lord Montague. Then she told the priest that Lady Isabella did not believe in the Church or its sacraments. She hinted that Lady Isabella was an occultist, a black magician.'

'And Rivers objected?'

'Naturally. He even threatened to leave her bedside. But Mathilda asked him two questions. First, why had that builder been summoned to the Hall, what had he built? Rivers couldn't answer. Secondly, Mathilda asked what had happened to the old woman, the witch from Candleton Village, who so mysteriously disappeared. This brought Rivers back to her bedside.'

Oliver picked up the poker from the hearth and stabbed at a log on the fire. It crumbled and broke in a shower of sparks.

Emma felt a chill of apprehension. The Hall was very quiet; she realised her brother was reaching the black heart of this matter.

'Mathilda claimed,' Oliver continued, 'that a secret chamber had been built in the Hall and that the witch whom Isabella had patronised had been her initiator into the black rites. Isabella had continued this, after she had murdered the old woman.'

'Murdered her?'

'That's what Mathilda said. Not only her, but the builder: they had both been killed to keep their mouths shut. Rivers found this difficult to accept but Mathilda challenged him. Why should a dying woman lie to a priest hearing her confession?'

'Didn't Rivers ask her why she had not revealed these matters earlier?'

'Of course, but Mathilda just scoffed, making the very sensible point that who would listen to her, the weak-minded daughter of Sir Henry? She had only survived because, like Rivers himself, she posed no danger to Lady Isabella. Rivers then mentioned justice, the need for the truth. Mathilda again mocked him and finished her confession.' Oliver got up, rubbing his hands. 'Mathilda revealed that she had taken matters into her own hands and murdered the Lady Isabella!'

Chapter 13

'Mathilda!' Emma exclaimed. 'A sickly old woman killing the powerful Lady Isabella!'

'Apparently.'

Oliver walked to the window. He was surprised that here he was, describing this great evil, yet nothing had happened; no interruptions. Was the ghost of Lady Isabella, that evil phantasm, as powerful as they thought? As if in answer he heard the jingle of harness and the clip-clop of hooves outside.

'Listen!'

Emma joined him at the window.

'I heard it as well,' she murmured. 'As if someone was riding?'

'Is anything wrong?'

Dr Meddlecott stood in the doorway. 'I thought I heard the sound of a horse. Did you?'

'We were just talking about that,' Emma said. She pointed back to the table. 'Oliver has transcribed Chaplain Rivers' confession. According to him, Mathilda killed Lady Isabella.'

'You mean the old woman who embroidered the tapestry?' Meddlecott paused; the jingle of harness and the clip-clop of hooves broke the silence. 'How can that happen?' he asked. 'I don't believe it. How can a Presence, that is incorporeal, make such physical manifestations?'

'I don't know,' Oliver replied. 'I've read every book on exorcisms and hauntings. Some experts believe it's all in our minds and that metaphysical forces simply play on this. Or that the Presence is like an invisible hand which slips into a glove giving it life and force.'

'But why that now?' Meddlecott countered.

'Listen!'

The mist suddenly shifted. The rider emerged. The horse was a dirty snow colour, its harness of red and gold, the saddle of polished leather with an ornamental crupper. The woman was dressed in dark burgundy. She sat as skilfully as any knight or cavalry man, tall and erect in the saddle,

The veil lifted from her face. Emma exclaimed in horror and turned away; Meddlecott stepped back but Oliver held those hideous eyes. Even though they were separated by a thick pane of glass and the herbaceous border round the outside of the house, those eyes seemed only inches from his own. This was no attempt to frighten, no physical manifestation to make him step back or think again. The gaze was cold and calculating like that of a swordsman who studies his opponent to get the worth of him. The pallid face was immobile, only the lips moved: Oliver felt the threat she was quietly mouthing. Her gaze never faltered and Oliver refused to look away.

The mists swirled in again; a log on the fire crackled. He gazed round. Emma had returned to her chair. Meddlecott, beside her, looked equally frightened. Oliver turned back to the window, but the apparition had vanished.

'She knows it will happen soon,' he declared.

'What will?' Meddlecott asked.

'The confrontation. She knows that and so do I. You asked how apparitions occur. I am not too sure whether there was a phantasm beyond the window or whether it was souls corresponding.'

'But does she really think?' Emma wiped the sweat from her hand on to the bodice of her gown. 'Does she really think that nothing will change? That the power of the Mass and prayer . . .?'

'As in life, so in death,' Oliver answered. 'Lady Isabella never gave a fig about God or man when she was Lady of this place so why should she now?' He picked up the confession. 'If Lady Mathilda could have proved everything she said, Lady Isabella would have been burnt or hanged but that never concerned her. So why now? The Church teaches our conscience is something we develop: when we die, we take it with us, but what if there is nothing to take?'

'She acts in death as she did in life?' Meddlecott added. 'The lady of the manor, high on her horse.'

'Precisely. Dominating anyone who opposed her, using whatever power at her disposal.'

'How did Mathilda kill her?' Emma asked.

'I thought,' Meddlecott added, 'Lady Isabella was seen leaving the Hall?'

'Rivers asked the same question. Apparently, on that fateful morning, Lady Isabella, as usual, told her grooms to prepare her horse. Mathilda seized her chance. She went into the Spanish Chamber, Lady Isabella's room, to have words. Mathilda must have been an incredibly strong-willed woman. Lady Isabella underestimated her, and that was a fatal error. Mathilda didn't confront her: she simply brought up the stirrup cup Lady Isabella always drank before her morning ride.'

'And it was poisoned?'

'Yes, something which acted very quickly. Mathilda didn't even wait to see the effects. Lady Isabella became ill, slouched in her chair. Mathilda then left, locking the door behind her.'

'But couldn't Lady Isabella have screamed for help?'

Emma tapped the table. 'Of course! The walls of the chamber are covered in Spanish leather, it would deaden any sound!'

'I doubt if Lady Isabella had much of an opportunity to scream,' Oliver continued. 'Death followed quickly. Mathilda returned and took Isabella's cloak, hat and veil; she apparently was the same size and height. She then swept into the stables and took the horse.' He shrugged. 'The rest would have been easy. Mathilda rides down to the mere, leaves the horse there, as well as Lady Isabella's veil, removes the cloak and walks back to the Hall as poor Mathilda.'

'But what happened to Isabella's corpse?'

'Rivers asked that but Mathilda was growing weaker, slipping in and out of consciousness. Rivers seized her hand and begged her. Mathilda replied: "Let her rot!" She then added in Latin: "*Per Hispaniam ad secretam*." '

'Through Spain to the secret,' Meddlecott translated. 'The same message was picked up off the tapestry. What can it mean?'

'I think I know,' Oliver replied. 'But I'd like to take a walk before it falls dark. Anyway,' he sighed, 'a few hours later Mathilda died. Rivers, shocked by what he had heard, retreated into himself. According to the records, a few months later he himself died, a sickly, old man, wandering in his wits. But, come.' Oliver rose and blew the candles out. '*Per Hispaniam ad secretam*.' Let us find out what it means.'

He went out into the hallway where the ever-solicitous Stokes brought him his hat and walking cane.

'Lady Alice,' the butler declared sonorously, 'is sleeping in her chamber. Ruth is with her.'

'We won't be long.' Oliver clapped the surprised butler on the shoulder. 'In fact, we'd like you to come with us. The Spanish Chamber, it's on the east wing of the house isn't it, at the back overlooking the gardens? Take us there please.'

Stokes raised his eyebrows but didn't object. He led them out through the back way. They crossed the bustling, steam-filled kitchens where cooks and scullions shouted at each other above the noisy clash of pans: they fell silent as Oliver passed.

'I'm afraid your presence, sir, well it's disconcerting and the servants are chattering.'

Oliver didn't reply. Emma tugged at the butler's sleeve.

'They are not frightened? They won't leave?' she asked.

'Not while I'm here, ma'am. I've told them they should trust

Lady Alice and the good priest. They are only to leave when I do, and that,' Stokes turned, gripping the lapels of his jacket like a parson ready to deliver a sermon, 'and that, ma'am, will never happen!'

He led them outside through the vegetable and herb gardens, around behind the east wing of the Hall. The ground here was frozen hard. Stokes explained that Lady Alice wished to extend the garden right down to the edge of the moat. He pointed to the windows in the different rooms.

'There.' He pointed through the faint tendrils of shifting mist. 'That small window is the one in the Spanish Chamber.'

'And there are other rooms next to it?' Oliver asked.

'Oh yes, sir, but much further along, as you can see.'

Oliver noticed the gap between the Spanish Chamber and the one to the right was much longer than the gap between it and the chamber on the left.

'And what's that?' Oliver asked and pointed to a square piece of wood. 'About four yards to the right of the Spanish Chamber as we look at it?'

Stokes peered up. 'Lord sir, I don't know but the guttering and brickwork have been changed so many times over the years.'

'Do you have any knowledge of joinery or carpentry, Stokes?'

'Some, sir, when I was a lad.'

'Well, I think,' Oliver replied peering up at that slat of wood, 'I think that the leather covering in the Spanish Chamber actually conceals an entrance to a secret room. I suspect that wooden slat can serve as its window.'

'There are such hideaways all over the house,' the butler replied. 'In the Elizabethan times, hiding-holes were carved out for the priests hiding from the sheriff's men, or so Sir Thomas told me. Some have been found, others are still hidden.' He gazed mournfully at the priest. 'But that room, sir, is a work of art. The leather coverings have never been taken down.'

'We won't have to take it all down,' Oliver replied, walking towards the kitchen door. 'It will be easier than that.'

Back in the hallway Stokes took their coats and hats.

'Are you certain of this?' Emma asked.

'I'm positive,' Oliver replied. 'Lady Isabella had a special chamber constructed. In the early sixteenth century.'

He continued as they followed Stokes up the stairs. 'When Catherine of Aragon came to marry first Prince Arthur and then Henry, Spanish customs and fashions became all the rage. When I studied in Valladolid I went to different places around the city. The use of such leather coverings was quite common. Other large houses in England must have had the same but many have now been destroyed.'

'And Lady Isabella would use this to disguise any secret door?'

Oliver smiled at Dr Meddlecott.

'I hope so. That's the only conclusion I can reach. Mathilda also knew this. I suspect that is where she dragged Isabella's corpse. Hence her phrase: "through Spain, to the secret".'

Just as they reached the landing leading down to the Spanish Chamber, Emma gripped her brother's arm.

'Is this safe?' she asked. 'Will we be the first to enter that room?'

'No, I don't think so. The Lady Margaret, some sixty years ago, also discovered the chamber. It will be interesting to see what she did.'

They opened the door. Emma held her breath. She was certain something would happen but the room was quiet. The light seeping through the small window only enhanced the serenity of the place.

'Bring some candles,' Oliver asked.

Stokes went outside and brought back candelabra from the tables along the gallery. Oliver waited until these had been lit.

'Now the chamber is boxlike. We have the window wall and the door wall. The room next to it,' he pointed to his right, 'is in close proximity. So, the secret chamber,' he gestured to the far wall, 'must be here. Behind the leather arras we will find the door.' He glanced over his shoulder at the painting. In the poor light he could make out Lady Isabella's features, her sharp nose and heavy-lidded eyes.

Oliver went to the wall and felt the thick spongy leather. 'It must have been both glued and fixed,' he said, 'to the plaster behind. What we need is some break in the leather. Notice the ripples, these could hide studs or catches.'

The others helped. At first the leather seemed seamless, as if it had been unrolled and cunningly fixed to the wall. Meddlecott found the first clasp in the far corner near the window: it was painted black and hidden behind a fold. Oliver crouched beside him and, running his fingers inside the leather crease, found the second. Emma brought across the candelabra.

'For God's sake, not too close!' she whispered. 'This is a work of art, Oliver!'

'There!'

Meddlecott pointed to a hairlike seam and, running his fingers along it, found another long line of studs just where the walls met. At first it was difficult to pull at them but eventually the first clasp came away, then the second. Now and again one of the clasps broke but, as the leather peeled off, Oliver realised it was a huge rectangle of moveable leather, about a yard across and four feet in length. He tapped behind it, raising clouds of dust, and felt the wood.

'This is the door!' Oliver exclaimed.

At last the whole leather portion came away. The wood beneath, once a polished brown, was now faded and cracked.

'A door in a wooden wall,' Meddlecott commented, sniffing at his fingers. 'Made out of good oak and strengthened with some form of polish.'

'But how does it open?'

Oliver felt the rim of the door. He made out the hinges, three in all. He took a candle and peered at these.

'They are relatively new,' he said. 'Certainly not medieval. I suspect Lady Margaret had the door strengthened and re-hung. But how do we open it?' He dug his nails into the thin edge. 'There's no handle, no keyholes.'

'Let me try?' Meddlecott offered. 'I once saw a medicine chest which worked something like this.' Meddlecott pressed firmly along the side of the door. 'It must be!' he whispered. He pressed hard at the bottom of the panel and they heard a click. Meddlecott started pressing very firmly further up. He must have hit a similar lock on the top, because with another click the door swung open.

'I am glad to see my medical experience has not been wasted.' Meddlecott crouched down looking at the catches. 'These are fairly recent. Look, the wood has been gouged. Whatever once held the door fast was removed and probably replaced with this by Lady Margaret, a locking mechanism which responds to pressure.'

The door was pulled back, the hinges still moving smoothly. Oliver peered in. The blackness smelt of a musty damp and he caught something acrid. The dust caught his nostrils and made him sneeze. He drew back, blowing his nose while Stokes went through the opening, a large candelabra before him. Emma passed another through.

'Goodness me!' The butler's voice sounded hollow. 'Oh, sir, you've got to see this!'

Oliver crept through. Two large candelabra now lit the room. The priest felt a chill of fear. The chamber was now dancing with shadows. The flickering light revealed a drawing on the ceiling and one on the far wall.

'Where's that wooden slat?'

Oliver looked behind him and caught a thin chink of light.

He went across and felt the edge of the wood. After an insistent knocking, it turned like a vent, allowing in fresh air and dull rays of light.

Emma and Meddlecott came in while Stokes went to fetch Lady Alice. For a while all three stared around in amazement.

The floor was of polished black wood; hangings had once covered the walls but these had now decayed and fallen in lumps. The drawing on the ceiling was similar to what Oliver had seen in many writings on black magic and witchcraft, a circle within a triangle, an open eye in the centre: around this were much faded symbols of the zodiac.

'That's probably the work of Lady Isabella,' Oliver said. He pointed to the inverted cross on the other wall. 'While that seems to have been repainted by Lady Margaret.'

The room had no furniture or any sign of habitation. It was Meddlecott who stumbled against the casket in a shadowy corner, lying against the wall in which the secret door had been built. He didn't open it but pushed it across.

The casket was about two yards long and a yard across, fashioned out of good polished oak, the lid held down by brass clasps. Meddlecott loosened them, pulled back the lid and lifted the gauze veils beneath. These crumbled in his hands.

The skeleton the cloths shrouded was much decayed. The lower jaw had split; the skull and other bones were yellowing and cracked. Any shroud or garment it had been dressed in for burial had long since rotted. Meddlecott said he could find no shards or scraps at the bottom of the coffin. Oliver knelt down, turning the grinning skull, staring into those empty eye sockets.

'Who is it?' Emma asked.

Oliver paused as Lady Alice came into the chamber. She exclaimed in surprise and, lifting the candelabra, stared around in wonderment.

'I never guessed this was here,' she said. 'Yet it now seems so obvious. No one ever dreamt of moving the Spanish leather arras.' She came over, stared down at the coffin then turned away, hand to her mouth. 'One of Lady Isabella's victims?' she asked.

'No, no.' Oliver got to his feet. 'I suspect it's Isabella herself. Over sixty-five years ago, the Lady of the Hall, Margaret Seaton, also found this chamber. She refurbished the painting on the wall and probably cleaned it out. The secret door was rehung with a fresh lock, the wooden slat replaced. Any medieval artefacts such as tapestries or carpets would be nothing but shards or piles of dust. In cleaning up the chamber, Lady Margaret probably removed its true horror, a place of diabolical sacrifice and midnight rites. She also found the remains of Lady Isabella. I'll explain more fully later,' he added, 'but I suspect that Mathilda Seaton killed the Lady Isabella, giving her a powerful poison and then dragged the corpse in here, and concealed it in a casket or arrow chest. The walls are thick and the leather coverings would have hidden any smell of putrefaction or decay. Now, Lady Margaret cleared the other artefacts away, but the remains of her ancestor, she placed in a coffin.'

Oliver was about to continue when the door swung shut with a crack. Some of the candles went out. Lady Alice stifled a scream. Meddlecott hurried to the door and began tugging at it but it wouldn't move. Oliver abruptly became aware of how cold the room had grown and that acrid smell, similar to saltpetre, turned to a pungent, distasteful odour. The few candles which remained alight danced and spluttered in the draught from the vent. Emma began to shiver, folding her arms. Lady Alice joined Meddlecott at the door, hammering with her fists, ignoring Meddlecott's entreaties to remain calm. They heard a rapping on the other side. The door clicked and swung open, Stokes pushed his head through.

'I wondered what had happened.'

'We should leave now,' Oliver insisted.

He held the door and let the others go through. He gazed one last time round the room, at the unlocked coffin, its rotting gauze bubbling out like froth on the edge of a dirty bath.

Oliver blew the candle out and joined the rest.

'I don't think we should stay here. Lady Alice, it's best if our good butler here keeps this room under lock and guard. Let's meet in my chamber.'

Once they were there, Lady Alice rang for her maid and told her to bring up tea and some scones. Oliver washed his hands in a bowl and looked out of the window. Dusk was falling.

'It's wise,' he declared, throwing the towel on to a chair, 'if we began immediately.'

'What?' Lady Alice asked.

'I really must say a Mass in that chamber. I know I said one out at the ruins earlier in the day but, in times of crisis, a priest can celebrate again. I would like Stokes and you, Dr Meddlecott, to remove the coffin. Take it down to the chapel and place it on the corpse stools before the high altar.'

'How dangerous is all this?' Lady Alice asked.

Oliver was about to reply when there was a knock on the door. Ruth came in with a tray of tea and scones. Meanwhile Stokes returned with the key to the Spanish Chamber.

Once Stokes and the maid had left Oliver sipped at the tea. He realised how the dust from that secret chamber had coated his lips and mouth as if, even in that short time, it wanted to leave its mark.

Meddlecott and Emma sat on the edge of the bed while Lady Alice paced up and down, ignoring Meddlecott's advice to sit and relax.

'Father, I asked you a question. Is this dangerous?' Lady Alice put her cup down, weaving her fingers together. 'Secret chambers, that dreadful woman's skeleton!'

'Why didn't the ghost intervene?' Meddlecott broke in. 'Why didn't Lady Isabella make her anger more fully felt?'

'I'm not too sure. What we found, well, it was of significance but nothing important, merely the dust of history, the relics of that evil woman. Lady Alice,' Oliver went on as he got up and, taking his hostess by the hand, firmly ushered her into a chair. 'Lady Alice.' He crouched beside her. 'Do you want to be rid of this evil?'

She rubbed her temples with her fingers. 'Of course I do but is it worth it?'

'Such an attitude,' Oliver continued, 'is dangerous. Lady Alice, if you trust me, and I beg you to do so, the worst thing that can happen is for you to ask me and my sister to leave, to give up the fight. I told you when I first came here: a haunting is a matter of intellect and will. That's the world Lady Isabella now lives in. Her intellect, her will and, more importantly, yours.'

Lady Alice looked up in surprise. Oliver caught the spurt of fear in her eyes.

'Can't you see,' he coaxed, 'you are doing what she wants? Think of the haunting as merely a malicious prank but still very dangerous. It's led to the deaths of two men, but Lady Isabella used them as a warning. They were, or made themselves, vulnerable. I don't know why they died. Lady Isabella was not really interested in them or in sweeping along passageways rattling chains or letting us hear the noise of spectral horsemen. These are only a means to an end: to weaken you, to overawe your intellect and, in the final resort, break your will. She doesn't wish to haunt Candleton. She wishes to haunt you, to possess you. She thinks the door to your soul is open as she found the way in to other holders of this Hall, with varying degrees of success. Thérèse in the seventeenth century; Lady Margaret some sixty years ago.'

Lady Alice sat, her face composed. She patted her stomach.

'Now and again,' she replied, as if speaking to herself, 'I feel the child stir and I think all is well.'

'But it isn't, is it Lady Alice? Please!' Oliver insisted. 'Shall I hear your confession?'

Emma got to her feet and grasped Meddlecott's wrist.

'In which case we should leave.'

'No.' Lady Alice shook her head and smiled through her tears. 'I want you here.' She took a deep breath. 'Yes, Father, it's best if you hear my confession.'

Oliver took his stole from the chest of drawers, put it on and pulled his chair alongside Lady Alice. He said a prayer and crossed himself.

'I don't know what to say. I . . .' Lady Alice murmured.

'Do you believe in Christ?'

'Of course!'

'Are you sorry for any sins you may have committed?'

'Of course.'

'Then, tell me, what bothers your conscience?'

'I, I . . .' Lady Alice looked up at the ceiling then at Dr Meddlecott.

Oliver waited. 'Speak as you think,' he urged.

'Father, I think I'm guilty of murder.'

Oliver ignored Emma's sharp intake of breath.

'Of whose murder?'

'My husband's.'

'Did you murder him?'

Lady Alice's face was now white and drawn, her lips one thin, bloodless line. The pupils of her eyes wandered as she stared at a point behind Oliver.

'In my mind,' she whispered, 'I have, many times. He was not the man I married. Oh, he was brave and strong but, when he drank and the house was quiet, the servants out of earshot, the cruelties would pour out like a filthy stream: the taunts, the insults. Sometimes he would take me, force me down on the floor. In the last few months he beat me, sometimes with his fists, and,' she glanced sideways at Meddlecott, 'at least on one occasion with a whip or riding crop.' She shook her head.

'Why?' Oliver asked.

'I know,' Lady Alice lifted a hand, 'what he did was wicked but he was angry at my childlessness. I think he has an illegitimate child somewhere in London. God knows who the poor unfortunate is. He also boasted about his prowess with another young lady in Norwich, then he'd sober up.

'At first I accepted his apologies. I did try to reason with him because, when he wasn't in his cups, then he was decent enough but, in the end.' She closed her eyes. 'It became one long, horrid nightmare.' She opened her eyes. 'On the evening before he was killed he beat me, forcing me on to the bed. Afterwards I lay in the darkness, Thomas beside me, snoring like a pig. I remember getting up and staring into the night.' She held Oliver's gaze. 'You talk about the intellect and the will. I tell you what, Father, I called on Hell, anything to help me. I wished he would die! If I had had the courage, or the strength, I would have taken a dagger and driven it through his heart. Heaven knows it was tempting enough.

'Despite my raging, I fell asleep in a chair. Thomas woke me the next morning. He was still in his cups, surly as ever. He told me to bring down a large goblet of claret as his stirrup cup. He said he would ride his horse then he'd come home and ride me. Do you know, Father?' She smiled thinly. 'I understand from Emma that you like Shakespeare. Well, I felt like Lady Macbeth taking that goblet down the stairs and out into the stable yard. I handed it to him. Thomas, he must have caught the look in my eyes: it's the only time I'd ever seen him look ashamed.' Lady Alice now balled her fists. ' "Die!" I thought. "Drink the wine and die! Fall off the horse, break your neck! Anything, just don't come back!" ' She paused. 'Father, I really wanted that, for him to die there and then.'

'Lady Alice.' Oliver chose his words carefully. 'That wine, was it untainted?'

'I told you, Father, I lacked the courage!'

'Or the will to evil,' Emma intervened.

'I don't know,' Lady Alice murmured. 'When my husband was killed, I felt like an assassin. I felt . . .' Then she put her face in her hands and sobbed quietly.

'And what do you feel now?'

Lady Alice lifted her head. 'Before God I feel no hatred for Thomas, only for what he did. I am sorry that he died.'

Oliver raised his hand and gave her absolution. Lady Alice looked up in surprise.

'Is it as simple as that, Father?'

Oliver shrugged and smiled. 'You were innocent of your husband's death. You felt hatred but, there again, he had hurt you deeply. You are sorry for your feelings.'

'But what about my penance?'

'I have some suggestions to make later,' Oliver replied. He rose and poured a cup of tea which he handed to her. 'I could offer to cook you a meal,' he teased. 'Then make you eat it. Now that would be a penance because I am an appalling cook.'

'I can vouch for that,' Emma cheerily agreed.

'What does Lady Alice mean by penance?' Meddlecott spoke up.

'It's not really penance,' Oliver said. 'But more reparation, putting things right. That has to be done here at Candleton. Hundreds of years ago, terrible acts were committed: murder, adultery, black magic and sorcery. Over the years the evil has been allowed to grow, batten and strengthen. Once, on a train outside Manchester, I saw how the air had grown black from smoke pouring out of the factory chimneys. I wondered if the spirit world is like that? Evil feeding on evil, polluting the soul. It's possible Lady Isabella's spirit fed on Sir Thomas's cruelty, Lady Alice's despair, her feelings of hate and rage.'

'Did she think she had a gateway into my soul?' Lady Alice asked.

'Possibly. Isabella was thrust, in secret, out of this life. She does not wish to leave Candleton and what better way than to possess the souls of others who live here? Sometimes, because of circumstances, she failed. But you?' Oliver spread his hands. 'In her eyes you were a perfect mirror of herself. She sensed your hurt, your hatred; she would grow strong on it. Sir Thomas's death had so much in common with Alain Montague's and others.

'Isabella thought she had found a way in but now the gate is shut, and we must drive her away for ever.'

Chapter 14

Oliver poured himself another cup of tea. He was aware of how quiet the house had become, an ominous stillness. Outside darkness had fallen.

'The exorcism must be performed tonight,' he said. 'Otherwise we will see manifestations and phenomena which would probably terrify everyone out of their wits. The Spanish Chamber must be cleansed and purified. A Mass must be said, and the exorcism will take place immediately afterwards.'

Oliver curbed his feelings of anxiety and panic: he realised the struggle was about to begin. Lady Alice's hand went to her lips as if she, too, was experiencing discomfort.

'I shall exorcise the house,' Oliver continued. 'In any other circumstances I would go to the chapel, but I think it best if I stay here. Lady Alice, I want you to ask the cooks and servants to stay in the kitchen downstairs. This gallery and the one leading from the Spanish Chamber must be kept strictly out of bounds. Whatever happens to me, whatever you feel, hear or experience, do nothing except pray.'

'Do you want us to deck the room with ivy, mistletoe and some garlic?' Meddlecott joked.

'No magic.' Oliver smiled. 'Just sit there with Lady Alice. Play a game of cards, talk about preparations for Christmas. Read Disraeli's latest novel or Gladstone's speeches, anything.'

'Won't you be in danger?' Emma asked.

'I would like to say I won't be,' Oliver replied. 'But, as long as I have faith and keep that faith it will end well. Now, come on, preparations have to be made.'

Two hours later, just as the hallway clock struck seven,

Oliver finished putting his vestments on. He approached the makeshift altar which Stokes had set up in the Spanish Chamber.

Oliver had spent most of the time reading his breviary and saying his prayers. Now, as he began the Mass for all those who had died at Candleton, he knew he was committed. He must see this matter through. Stokes had done a good job: the white cloths, the missal from the church, candlesticks, offertory cruets, paten and chalice.

'I could stay with you, sir,' the butler offered.

Oliver refused. 'The best thing you can do, Stokes, is stay downstairs and keep everyone calm.'

'Will anything happen?'

'I would like to say it won't but, unfortunately, yes, it will.' Oliver lifted his hand. '*In nomine Patris et Filii et Spiritus Sancti, Amen.*'

Oliver moved swiftly through each phase of the Mass: the prayers for the dead; the readings; moving to the right side of the altar for the gospel and then, pouring the wine into the chalice, he lifted it up, concentrating on the rite.

As he reached the consecration, Oliver realised how cold the room had grown. The door to the secret chamber was open: gusts of chill air came out, followed by the stench of rottenness. He leant over the bread and wine saying the sacred words and then he heard it, even as he lifted the chalice, the whispering, the subdued chatter as if there were people in the secret chamber quietly plotting. The door to the chamber shut then opened violently. Again a rush of icy air which made him flinch then gag at the terrible odour filling the room.

The whispering grew, interspersed by a chuckle, low, malevolent, as if he was being mocked.

'Stop your canting, priest!'

The words came from the darkness to his left.

'Stop this canting and go! Take your preaching and

your magic! All is mine, always has been, always will!'

Oliver prayed the words of the consecration. He turned to give the blessing and, as he did, something floated in front of him, blocking his view, like a bat or bird skimming through the air. Oliver closed his eyes, blessed himself and finished the Mass.

As he divested, saying the words laid down by the rite, the chattering and whispering from the chamber ended. Oliver knelt at the prie-dieu. He took his breviary out, picked up the small stoup of holy water and sprinkled it. The water smacked against the leather tapestry. Oliver quoted the blessing from memory, asking for the presence of Christ and his angels to remove and destroy all evil. He then rose and went into the secret chamber. He did not bring a candle but again repeated the rite. Nothing happened. He was about to leave when he felt himself shoved, banging his head against the half-open door. He staggered back into the Spanish Chamber, the holy water stoup fell from his hand and, before he could put it right, most of it had splashed out on to the floor.

For a while Oliver nursed his sore head. He went to pick up the stoup and froze: a pair of polished boots of cordovan leather and the hem of a red damask skirt blocked his move. He looked up. The woman was the same, though dressed in different attire, the gown ringed by a small lace ruff, a silver chain belt around her waist, her cloak and hood black as night. Oliver gazed at the contemptuous look on that narrow, lean face.

'Get thee gone!' The words came like a snarl, deep and low.

'In Christ's name!' Oliver retorted.

The woman's hand came back and he glimpsed the riding crop she held. Oliver closed his eyes and put his hand up but nothing happened.

When he opened his eyes, the chamber was empty and cold; the candles had been extinguished, only traces of that awful stench remained. Oliver put his face in his hands.

'Stop it! Stop it!' he said quietly to himself. 'Do not be afraid. Phantasms and tricks! Nothing else.'

He put his hand to the floor and felt something sticky and wet. At first he thought it was some wine Stokes might have spilt but, after he'd lit the candles on the altar, he saw the stain was blood, dark and red. He went to wipe his hands but the blood had gone: black, buzzing flies swarmed over the stain on the floor. Oliver lashed out with his foot. He nearly lost his balance and, when he steadied himself, one hand against the altar, the flies and blood had gone. Oliver recalled the words of a Franciscan who had assisted him in his training.

'It's all tricks,' the old man had said. 'Just like in the Scriptures where the Devil threw a man into a fit or pretended to be a dog. If you become frightened, you lose faith and, if you lose faith, then there's nothing you can do.'

Oliver went out into the passageway and brought back fresh candles. He composed himself and recited the exorcism proper: a general invocation to the Trinity, to Christ, His Blessed Mother and all the saints and angels in Heaven. Halfway through it he heard the sound of pounding on the stairs as if someone in a temper was banging their feet at every step.

'I told you!' The voice echoed like a clap of thunder. 'I told you to stop and to leave! You trespass where you should not.'

Oliver continued his prayers. The pounding died away. Other manifestations followed: a child's voice; a woman singing; another screaming; the crack and fall of a whip. From the secret chamber came an incantation. The voice was so deep and hollow, Oliver couldn't decide whether it was male or female but, as he prayed the litany, the voice mimicked and mocked what he was doing.

Oliver paused and sprinkled holy water to all four corners of the room. As if in answer came the sound of a person retching and vomiting. The priest did his best to ignore the urgent gasps and foetid odour which followed.

He moved out into the gallery. Stokes had lit a few candles, shadows danced along the walls. Through a window at the far end Oliver glimpsed the moon. Suddenly a shape blocked it out, drifting towards him. A woman, not Isabella, dressed in medieval garb. She came closer, like someone in a dream, mouth open, hands outstretched, her face vivid with fear. He stood his ground and the apparition disappeared. Others followed: the young man he had seen outside, one hand on his knife, the other clutching at his throat, his face contorted in agony as if he fought against the poison he had just drunk. Somewhere else a dog began to howl, low and menacing. Oliver glanced to his right. Up the side staircase slipped a dark shape, long and darting like the shadow of a wolf. Oliver tensed. A throaty snarl broke the silence, the shape was loping towards him, red-eyed, white-toothed, then it disappeared. Outside the clop of hooves echoed insistently, as horses neighed and whinnied amidst shouts and exclamations.

Oliver walked down the gallery quietly reciting the words of the exorcism. He paused. Floating down the gallery, its feathered wings silently beating the air, came an owl, flying silently towards him. He could see its rounded face and cruel yellow beak, the talons stretched as if it was swooping for the kill. The priest closed his eyes and, when he looked again, the phantasm had disappeared.

He blessed the gallery and continued up a flight of side stairs on to the gallery to his chamber and that of Lady Alice. The candlelight filled the vaulted passageway with shifting shadows which played tricks on his mind. Intangible forms, unreal shapes danced around him. Sometimes the air turned hot like the blast from an open furnace only to turn savagely cold. Smells and odours changed and mingled: rushes green and fresh, sprinkled with spring herbs, the foul smell of a midden or the rank miasma from some forest marsh. Footsteps clattered alongside or behind him. Shapes loomed up: a man in a cowl, only the side of his face visible in the dim candlelight.

Oliver reached the end of the gallery and came back. At the top of the main staircase he blessed the hallway below. He turned and, as he did so, the sleeve of his jacket caught the flame of the candle. The fire licked greedily at the wool but, when Oliver drew away, beating his arm, he could feel no heat and the fire disappeared.

He re-entered the gallery leading to the Spanish Chamber and found it changed. The panelling had gone, the walls were covered in plaster, rushes underfoot. A pale-faced servant girl, blood seeping out of the corner of her mouth, staggered out of the Chamber, cowering at the shrieks and yells coming from within.

'You stupid wench! Feckless noddlepate!'

Oliver walked on fearful lest he trip or fall, desperate that these images did not overcome him, stifling his mind, cut off the prayers he was reciting.

By the time he reached the door to the Spanish Chamber everything was as it should be. He went in and knelt before the crucifix. He took a deep breath as he intoned, as loudly as he could: 'I exhort you evil spirit, in the name of Christ Jesus, to depart from this place!'

Behind Oliver the Presence hovered. Its consciousness was only aware of a place where it had once lusted, plotted and schemed. This was, as it always had been, its secret place, the root of its continued existence here. The Presence was also aware of the sins it had sown here and the black harvest of cruelty, death and destruction. Now all its being, all its malevolence was directed at this priest, kneeling before his paltry altar, whose prayers and incantations were breaking up its world.

The Presence was growing fearful of other feelings, sensations and thoughts. The souls of others, once in its power, were now no longer part of its experience: they had left, travelling on over that distant rim of light. Others were now intruding. The Presence caught snatches of music which provoked memories of its life before death: hymns, psalms. These in turn caused apprehension and guilt for crimes committed. Worse, those pillars of blue-gold fire on the edge of its awareness had now grown stronger and closer. In them the Presence recognised faces from its previous life. Monks cast out of their living: Brother Stephen the Novice Master; Brother Norbert the Infirmarian, Prior Anselm, Brother John the Sub-Prior. What had they to do with its world, its desires, its will?

The priest was to blame. His meddling, his prayers, his discovery of the truth and the solace and comfort offered to the woman. If only it still could break through, really manifest its power, violence and determination to stay and have its way . . .

Oliver, unaware of the force gathering around him, reached that part of the rite in which the celebrant must call upon the spirit or being against which the exorcism was being directed. All manifestations and phenomena had now ceased. The house lay silent. Oliver wiped the sweat from his brow on the cuff of his sleeve.

'I adjure you!' he declared. 'I adjure you, evil spirit, by what name are you called?'

'Isabella!' The reply was hoarse, bellowed from behind him.

'Isabella Seaton?' he asked.

'The same!'

'By what right do you stay here?'

'By my own will and determination.'

'For what purpose?'

'You know that, don't mock me, priest!'

'You have sinned grievously,' Oliver continued remorselessly. 'You committed dreadful murder. You betrayed your husband, assassinated his sons and, when it suited you, arranged the death of Alain Montague. You persecuted and you harassed. You coveted, then you stole what was not yours!'

'It was mine, always mine, always will be!'

Oliver felt the chill blast on his neck, the urge to turn round but he resisted: he would adhere to the rite. He would not allow his will to be dictated to by this evil Presence.

'This haunting must end!'

'Never!' The denial was spat out like the lash of a whip cracking the air.

'I adjure you in the name of Christ Jesus to go. To continue your journey, to face your sins, to leave this place and all who dwell in it at peace!'

'Never! Look at me priest!'

Oliver recited the 'Our Father' aware of the baleful Presence all around him, threatening him, stifling his thoughts, weakening his will. Nevertheless, at the same time he quietly rejoiced. The Presence had shown the full extent of what powers it had. He struggled to finish his prayer.

'All is finished!' Oliver stated. 'Your sins have been exposed, reparation will be done!' He lifted his hand to make the final blessing.

'At least face me, priest!'

Oliver lowered his hands and got to his feet. He turned. The apparition in the doorway was dressed in dark-purple velvet. The face was young and tender, its skin white and pink, the eyes and mouth warm and alluring.

'Please!' The word echoed in his brain, soft and sibilant. 'Please! There is no harm in me!'

'I adjure you!' Oliver raised his hand. 'I call on St Michael the Archangel, all the angels of God and the saints of Heaven to assist me. I adjure you in the name of the Father and of the Son Incarnate.'

Oliver paused: the shape in the doorway changed like smoke curling above a fire. The face became older, crinkled, the eyes venomous, the mouth curled in a snarl. The apparition hurtled towards him.

'I adjure you!' Oliver stood his ground and continued the solemn blessing. 'In the name of the Holy Spirit.' He closed his eyes. 'And of the Blessed Virgin Mary . . .'

The Presence was in agony, writhing and turning in its own private hell: its consciousness was disintegrating and, with it, the world in which it dwelt. The pillars of blue-gold fire were now very close. Like poles in a fence, they drew together, closing round it, sealing it in like a trap. The faces in each pillar were quite distinct, the lips were moving in prayer, their eyes watching her, Lady Isabella Seaton. Hymns and chants filled the void and, beneath that, a growing, insistent chorus that she'd desist and go with them.

The Presence flung itself about in one silent scream. The pillars were now joining and closing in. Like someone drowning her will ebbed and weakened. She would have to go where they wished to take her. The sky above was now shot with gold. All dark images had disappeared. She was aware of the priest, his will fixed in that solemn adoration and blessing. If only she could lash out! If only she could break through! If only she could possess what was hers!

Oliver stood so tense, the pains coursed down his back and legs. Eyes tightly closed, he proceeded to the end of the exorcism. He tried to close his mind to the cacophony of sound which now rang through the house, crashing in the gallery outside, pounding on the stairs. Screams and shrieks shattered the silence.

He opened his eyes. The shape had gone but Lady Isabella's portrait had broken loose, thrown with great force on to the floor. The candlelight was dancing in the piece of glass covering the tapestry. Suddenly this was flung from the wall, as if dragged by invisible hands, and fell with a crack, smashing to smithereens. The door to the secret chamber was opening and shutting. Foul smells flowed and ebbed. The candle flames sprang up like lighted jets of gas, turning blue before subsiding.

Other sounds and images thrust themselves upon him: his name was being called. He did not know whether it was Emma, Arthur or his parents. Then silence.

Oliver let out his breath in one long gasp and jumped as the door to the secret chamber slammed shut. He lowered himself into a chair, hands joined, and waited. Was this a respite or the end? He forced himself to relax before getting to his feet and staggering out on to the gallery.

The place was a shambles. Pictures had been pulled from the walls, chairs and tables overthrown. Part of the stair carpet had been rucked up and a candle lay burning in the corner, its flame licking the wall. He went over and stamped it out. Was it the end?

Oliver went back into the Spanish Chamber. He recited the Requiem three times before leaning down to kiss the holy relic on the altar.

'Lord Jesus,' he whispered. 'I give You thanks that it is over. The Mass is ended.'

'*Deo gratias*. Thanks be to God!'

Oliver turned. The voices had spoken in unison firmly, calmly, like a chorus of priests at a Solemn High Mass. Oliver walked to the window and pushed it open. The sky was cloud-free; it was not so cold as before. He walked out to the top of the stairs leading down to Lady Alice's room.

'Priest!'

The voice was so soft it caught Oliver unawares. One hand on the banister, he turned. Lady Isabella stood behind him, so close she could have kissed him on the neck. He stared in horror.

'Priest!' The eyes were no longer venomous but pleading, the voice was a soft whine like that of a spoilt child.

'Get you gone!' Oliver spoke before he could think.

He watched the face push closer. He closed his eyes and heard a whisper: 'We must be gone! We can tarry no longer!'

The words were quaint, spoken in old-fashioned English and, when Oliver looked again, the apparition had vanished.

'Oliver!'

Emma stood at the foot of the stairs.

'Oliver, what on earth has been happening? Have you seen the gallery?'

He hurried down. The gallery was like the one he had left: furniture overthrown, paintings torn off the walls. The carpet had been kicked up, plants and vases overturned, spilling their contents out on to the floor. At the far end a thrown candelabra had started a small fire but Stokes had doused this.

'How is Lady Alice?'

'Oh, she's well,' Emma replied. 'We heard the terrible noise and screams but William, I mean Dr Meddlecott, told us not to leave the chamber.'

Oliver followed her into Lady Alice's bedroom. She was seated at a table near the window, Meddlecott at her side.

'My good fellow.' Meddlecott ushered him to a chair. 'I'm tempted to say you look as if you've seen a ghost!'

'I would love some tea,' Oliver said. 'Yes, tea and something sweet.'

Lady Alice pulled at the bell rope.

'Stokes,' she said as soon as the butler appeared. 'Go down and tell the servants not to be frightened.' She glanced at Oliver. 'Everything is finished?'

Oliver nodded.

'And ask Ruth to bring up some tea and cake for Father Oliver, Stokes.'

'There's a terrible mess outside,' Stokes said lugubriously.

'It will wait,' Lady Alice replied. 'We will have it all cleaned up tomorrow.'

Stokes sighed heavily and closed the door. Oliver succinctly described what had happened. Meddlecott just shook his head.

'If I told my friends in London . . .' he said. He saw the look on Oliver's face. 'No, I'll keep quiet. Emma has told me these exorcisms are done under the greatest possible secrecy. But what really happened?'

'I can't really explain,' Oliver admitted. 'The Church's theology on life after death is so meagre. All I can describe is what I did. I suspect that Lady Isabella's soul stayed here after death, locked in some metaphysical moment of time and space, aware of only her own determination to have her way and not let go. She drew her power from the evil she did. As Shakespeare puts it: "the evil that men do lives after them". She also exploited whatever evil occurred here.'

'But why now?' Lady Alice asked. 'I mean, did she draw strength from me? From my thoughts?'

'Possibly,' Oliver replied. 'But she also drew strength from secrecy, ancient sin, unatoned evil. Once that was shattered, she made herself vulnerable to other forces, other powers.'

'Are you saying she disappeared like a wisp of smoke?' Meddlecott asked.

'No, she was more like a ship whose mooring rope has been cut: she started a journey which really should have begun centuries ago. She will be brought to a state where she will be made to confront the evil she did.'

'And?'

'That will be a matter between her and God. If she remains obstinate in her sin, that will be her Hell. If she wishes to purge herself, then the journey will continue, God will have mercy on her.'

'Is it really ended?' Lady Alice asked.

'It is ended,' Oliver confirmed. 'And it will remain ended, provided you fulfil certain conditions.'

He paused as Ruth brought in a tray of tea and cake. Once she had served and left, Oliver seized his cup and, despite the scalding heat, drank greedily.

'Ah!' He closed his eyes. 'There must be tea in Heaven!'

'And date and walnut cake,' Emma teased, passing the plate.

'What you must do,' Oliver continued between mouthfuls, 'is have the remains of Lady Isabella buried in consecrated ground. I can do that for you tomorrow morning. The secret chamber must be utterly destroyed, the wall taken down. The rest can be hung in leather so that the style is not broken.

'I recommend Mathilda's tapestry be put in the church. Anything involving Lady Margaret or Lady Isabella must be removed from the Hall and destroyed. The Spanish Chamber can become a chapel of repose. Masses should be celebrated there in reparation as well as for those who have died here.' He put his cup down. 'I would suggest that some fund for good work be established in reparation or atonement. After a while, now the fire has gone out, the wisps of smoke which remain will disappear for ever.'

'One thing I didn't confess.' Lady Alice spoke up and, as she put her own cup down, her hands trembled. 'Was that while my husband was alive I, I, well . . .' She played with a ring on her finger. 'I met, I liked very much a distant kinsman, Lord Ralph Mowbray.' She blushed and patted her swelling stomach. 'Nothing untoward ever happened in either thought, word or deed but . . .'

'Ah, that's my penance,' Oliver broke in. 'You are to stop punishing yourself. Sir Thomas is dead, God rest him. You, Lady Alice, are carrying his child but you are a free woman. You must not think that the Furies will continue to pursue you.'

'And will you leave now?' Meddlecott asked anxiously.

'No, no, you can't!' Lady Alice declared. 'Christmas is coming. Surely, Father, you can stay?'

Oliver glanced at Emma. 'Yes . . .' he began.

'We would love to,' Emma intervened. She blushed and avoided Oliver's gaze. 'We really should ensure that all stays well.'

* * *

Kitty Edelman, a young drab who had hired a chamber in Benfleet's old house in Seven Dials, paused halfway down the stairs. She had heard rumours about this place. How Benfleet had lured street-walkers like herself, taken their money, killed them and buried their corpses in the cellar. How the house had become haunted by its previous owner.

The new landlord had cleaned and painted some of the old house but then became tired of it, letting out the chambers, as Benfleet had done, for a few pennies a week.

Kitty looked down at her black, polished, laced boots and flounced her dress. If she earned enough money tonight perhaps, before the month was out, she could secure a better place. She glanced up the darkened stairwell. Benfleet's house smelt rank and foetid. Moreover, this was the second time she had heard eerie sounds and glimpsed strange sights such as that figure, flitting like a shadow, dressed in a shabby, yellow dress with a red kerchief round her face. And why was the place always so cold? And hadn't Bridget, one of her companions, complained about strange noises at night? Kitty sniffed. She was about to continue down the stairs when she heard the ominous creaking coming from a room somewhere at the top of the house. Kitty was unsure, but it sounded like a rocking chair being pushed wildly backwards and forwards.

Satan's Fire

P. C. Doherty

In 1303 the Old Man of the Mountain remembers back to when he nearly killed Edward of England almost thirty years before. He never forgets his prey – and now decides to release an imprisoned leper knight to avenge old grievances.

One windswept evening a few months later two nuns are hurrying to their mother house in York when they smell the sickly odour of burning human flesh. Rounding the corner, they confront the macabre sight of a man being hungrily consumed by a roaring fire.

News of this grisly death meets Edward I of England as he arrives in York for secret negotiations with the leaders of the military Order of the Temple. His unease deepens for, as he enters the city, a would-be regicide attempts to murder him. When the assassin, wearing the livery of the Templar Order, is found dead – having been engulfed by a mysterious fire – Edward immediately enlists the help of his Keeper of the Secret Seal, Sir Hugh Corbett, to investigate.

0 7472 4905 9

HEADLINE

The House of Crows

Paul Harding

London Coroner Sir John Cranston and his faithful clerk, Brother Athelstan, return to pit their wits against a bloody murderer and the assassin in the House of Crows.

It's the spring of 1380 and the Regent John of Gaunt needs money supplies for his war against the French. Unfortunately the members of parliament at Westminster are proving especially stubborn – and the Regent's cause is not aided when some representatives from the shire of Shrewsbury are foully murdered. John of Gaunt orders Cranston to find the assassin before he loses every chance of obtaining the taxes he requires.

On top of that, Sir John and Brother Athelstan have their own problems. Someone is stealing cats from the streets and alleyways of Cheapside. And terrified parishioners are insisting that a devil incarnate is prowling around the parish of St Erconwald's, claiming innocent lives . . .

0 7472 4918 0

HEADLINE